Lost Amusement Parks of the Hudson Valley

Wesley Gottlock
Barbara H. Gottlock

©2016 by the authors Wesley and Barbara H. Gottlock. All rights reserved.

ISBN: 978-1537298474

Contents

Acknowledgements   2

Introduction   5

Map   12

1. Electric Park at Kinderhook Lake   13

2. Woodcliff Pleasure Park   51

3. Orange Lake   79

4. Indian Point Park   108

5. Fort George Amusement Park   139

6. Here and There   172

Lost Amusement Parks of the Hudson Valley

Acknowledgements

The geographical scope of this book led us to many new and interesting places, from Kinderhook Lake all the way down the Hudson Valley to the northern reaches of Manhattan. Along the way we were fortunate to meet scores of people who were not only helpful but downright encouraging as well. Their passion for local history was contagious.

Thanks to John Ansley, Head of Archives and Special Collections at the Cannavino Library at Marist College in Poughkeepsie, for generously sharing material relating to the Woodcliff Pleasure Park. Carney Rhinevault, Hyde Park Town Historian and author, provided valuable contacts and material for Woodcliff as well. We thank him and his talented wife, artist Tatiana Rhinevault, whose wonderful sketches of Woodcliff's past became useful. In Poughkeepsie, the Dutchess County Historical Society provided some interesting information on Woodcliff as did Lynne Lucas of the Adriance Branch of the Poughkeepsie Library. The former existence of the Woodcliff Pleasure Park was brought to our attention by *Hudson Valley Ruins* co-author Rob Yasinsac. Thanks, Rob. Also meriting kudos for Woodcliff are Charles H. Wheeler for sharing the Winslow estate photographs, Christopher Pryslopski from the Hudson Valley Institute, Hunt Auctions, and Abigail Herlihy for her insights into the transformation of the Winslow property.

Electric Park at Kinderhook Lake was brought to our attention by Larry Laliberte. Larry also braved an ice storm

Acknowledgements

to meet with us and share his wonderful postcard collection for which we are most grateful. The Columbia County Historical Society deserves special mention. The director Diane Shewchuk and her helpful staff were very generous in our several trips there while we perused Electric Park's vintage slide collection and other material. The input from Michael Cooney, the North Chatham Library, George Vollmuth, and Dominick Lizzi is appreciated.

The chapter on the amusement park at Indian Point would not have been possible without gaining access to the William J. Burke History Room in the Town of Buchanan. For that we thank Mayor Sean Murphy. A huge thanks to Brian Vangor for his interest in our project and particularly the chapter on Indian Point. Brian's passion for history and the Hudson Valley are evident in his volunteer work and in the marvelous photographs he has taken over the years. Thanks to Curt Pratt for introducing us to Brian. Robert Ferguson was kind enough to share some Indian Point material with us as well.

We would like to thank our friends Carla Decker and Gary Ferguson for sharing their postcard collections with us, particularly of the amusement park at Orange Lake. The local history room of the Newburgh Library was, as always, very useful.

The story of the Fort George Amusement Park was difficult to piece together. It took the help of numerous people and agencies to reconstruct some of its history. Cole Thomas provided information and contacts that proved invaluable. One of these contacts was Jason Minter. Jason's postcard collection filled a void in the chapter. On a day of horrid weather, we found warmth and welcome in his delightful *Indian Road Cafe* in the Inwood section of Manhattan. A special thank you goes to Fred Dahlinger of Wisconsin whose knowledge of amusement parks and their attractions is nothing short of amazing. Fred's input added much to the chapter. Duane Perron of Oregon provided fascinating information about one of Fort George's carousels which will soon be back in operation. Kudos also go to Washington Heights/Inwood historian James Renner, the New York Historical Society, and Kathy McCauley of the Bronx Historical Society.

Thanks again to Brian Gottlock for the thankless job of proofreading much material. Others deserving of mention are the Library of Congress, Howard Shack, and Bob McGlaughlin. We apologize for any omissions and we're certain there are some.

Introduction

Who doesn't have fond recollections of summer days and evenings at an amusement park? Where else have the five senses been so thoroughly stimulated? The thrill of the rides, the excitement of the midways, the seemingly limitless entertainment, and the food are ingrained in our memories. Add the natural ingredients of the Hudson River's scenery and its water routes to glorious river towns and the result is a perfect combination. This book's scope encompasses a number of amusement parks located along the Hudson River Valley during the first half of the 20th century. While the major parks of the time such as Coney Island, Palisades Amusement Park, Rye Playland, and Freedomland have been documented extensively, the following pages pay homage to some of the smaller parks which dotted the map from just south of Albany downriver to northern Manhattan. They became playgrounds for millions of valley residents and New York City visitors alike by providing wholesome entertainment in beautiful settings.

Amusement parks have been defined as the generic name for outdoor places of recreation, usually with a collection of rides and other attractions, to entertain large groups. It is interesting to note their development over time even before they appeared along the Hudson River Valley.

Lost Amusement Parks of the Hudson Valley

Amusement parks are by no means an American phenomenon. Bakken in Copenhagen is generally regarded as the world's first amusement park. It was founded in 1583 by a woman named Kirsten Piil when she bought property with natural springs. Initially people came for the healing power of the springs but soon various forms of games and entertainment evolved. Jugglers, court jesters, and magicians performed. Elementary games of chance became a standard. Incredibly, Bakken is still a hugely popular modern amusement park today.

During the 17th century pleasure gardens (also called pleasure parks) made their debuts throughout Europe. Space was set aside for citizens seeking relief from everyday life. The earliest pleasure gardens consisted of beautifully landscaped walking paths with flower beds and fountains. Diversions included bowling, tennis, and shuffleboard, among others. Food and drink concessions became standard. Beer gardens developed. But by the 18th century people were seeking more variety in the parks. Circus acts, balloon rides, and crude "thrill" rides became the lure.

It wasn't until the 1873 World's Fair in Vienna that the focus of the parks changed from mere relaxation to rides and attractions that offered even greater thrills. Fun houses, "pleasure wheels" (the precursor to the Ferris wheel), midways, and rudimentary roller coasters made appearances. But the World Columbian Exposition of 1893 (also known as The Chicago World's Fair) in Chicago had an even greater impact. Over six months, its 27,000,000 visitors (almost half the U.S. population at that time) were able to observe over 200 structures of classical architecture, industrial prototypes, cultural exhibits, and

Introduction

the latest advancements in amusements. "Modern" midways, new concessions, and rides were introduced. But the grand attraction was the debut of the Ferris wheel. Previous to the fair, most pleasure wheels were manually driven while spinning a few dozen riders around its axis. The planners of the fair put out a challenge for the creation of a unique ride to outdo the Eiffel Tower, which had been the star of the 1889 World's Fair in Paris. George Ferris, a construction engineer from Illinois, accepted the dare. Ferris went about designing an "observational" wheel, a sensation and the centerpiece of the fair, and the aptly named "Ferris" wheel soon became a fixture in amusement parks. The wheel was mammoth; with its 264-foot diameter, the wheel spun into the air around its 46-ton axle. Each of the three dozen gondolas could hold up to 60 people. Filled, the Ferris wheel held 2,160 riders, an astounding number. At 50 cents per ticket, a sold-out ride generated over $1,000, a very significant sum for the era.

The fair spawned other amusement parks around the country, not the least of which was Steeplechase Park in Coney Island in 1897. Coupled with Luna Park, the wild success of Coney Island fueled the rise of amusement parks through its "golden era" into the late 1920s.

Around the turn of the 20th century, entrepreneurs, duly noting the success of Coney Island, cast their eyes on the Hudson Valley and with good reason. The valley's character was changing. Fewer residents worked in agrarian pursuits. With the Industrial Revolution in full swing, many sought jobs in manufacturing, often leaving the workers with time off on the weekends. Likewise, New York City's burgeoning population created a need for respites away from tenement life and the city's sweltering summers. The demand for entertainment and escape was tremendous. Three factors made opportunities especially appealing in the Hudson Valley: steamships, trolleys, and the natural majestic beauty of the Hudson Valley. With numerous steamers already plying the river, masses seeking fresh air and fun could be transported to the valley's key cities and locales such as Newburgh, Kingston, Poughkeepsie, Indian Point, West Point, and Albany.

Trolley lines, no longer horse-drawn but electrified, were already in place and were often extended to carry the throngs to the doorsteps of newly created parks. The era of "electric parks" (or "trolley parks") had begun. The Electric Park at Kinderhook Lake was a perfect example. An inter-urban railway company brought thousands of weekend visitors to Electric Park which was mid-way between the cities of Albany and Hudson, its two terminuses. Electric companies and railroad companies collaborated to form these parks as will be discussed later in more detail. Adding to the allure, the Hudson River provided the scenic beauty which made a day's excursion up the river from New York City or down from Albany a lovely experience in itself.

The rise of amusement parks in the valley was gradual but steady. Attendance grew year by year as word spread about the delights found in the parks. Most of the amusement parks covered in these pages offered standard features such as Ferris wheels, a midway, a "shoot the chutes", a roller coaster, games of chance, a penny arcade, an aerial swing, whip rides, and a dance hall, in addition to other thrill rides and food concessions. But most offered something unique to provide visitors with a varied menu.

Introduction

Electric Park at Kinderhook Lake and the amusement park at Orange Lake in Newburgh offered myriad water related activities in and around their lovely lakes in addition to their ride attractions. To cool the patrons at Indian Point Park in Buchanan and Woodcliff Pleasure Park in Poughkeepsie, two of the largest pools along the East Coast were constructed. Woodcliff also boasted the world's highest and faster roller coaster. The Fort George Amusement Park in northern Manhattan provided enough entertainment to rival Coney Island and the Palisades Amusement Park. Most parks offered some type of live entertainment ranging from opera to vaudeville to major sporting events. Several offered spectacular fireworks displays. The Mount Beacon Incline Railway brought passengers to the mountain's summit for the most splendid views of the river and the Hudson Highlands. There was something for everyone.

While amusement parks were hugely popular for the first two decades of the 20th century, extraneous events gradually led to the demise of many. (These events will be discussed in detail later.) Many parks were simply neglected and eventually abandoned. Others succumbed to fires. The "Golden Age" of roller coasters peaked in the late 1920s with the Blue Streak roller coaster at Woodcliff Pleasure Park reigning supreme even though the Cyclone at Coney Island grabbed most of the headlines. Around this time roller coasters had become amusement parks' centerpieces.

With the Great Depression in full gear and World War II around the corner, amusement parks slid into a lull that would last until the debut of theme parks. Frontier Town in North Hudson (1952) and Storytown USA (1954) in the

Lost Amusement Parks of the Hudson Valley

Adirondack region were among the first of the new wave. But the debut of Disneyland in Anaheim, California on July 15, 1955 created a new standard for amusement parks. Amusement parks once again rose in popularity through the 1960s and 1970s (many qualifying as theme parks) culminating with the "coaster wars" in which each new venue tried to outdo its competitors in the speed, height, twists, and turns of its steel tracks.

Like the days of men's straw hats and vests and ladies' floor length dresses and parasols harkening back to simpler times, it is sad to note that virtually nothing remains of the once glorious amusement parks of the Hudson Valley. While Kinderhook Lake and Orange Lake are still beautiful recreational lakes where boaters and fishing enthusiasts can enjoy a day's outing, precious little remains to remind of us of the steamboat excursions, the trolley rides, the thrill rides, the beautiful flowered paths, and the continuous entertainment. The Woodcliff Pleasure Park is now the grounds for part of Marist College's athletic fields and student housing. Though one of the larger parks discussed in this book at least in the range and size of its attractions, it is interesting to note that Woodcliff leaves behind the least amount of images, records, and accounts of its interesting 14-year existence. Most area residents now associate Indian Point as a place where huge nuclear reactors loom over the river and generate electricity for hundreds of thousands. Few remember that the very same acreage was a playground for millions for many years. The Fort George Amusement Park in northern Manhattan is now part of Highbridge Park. Kingston Point is now public park land. While most of these venues have been put to good use, only the Mount Beacon Incline Railway has a chance to return to its

Introduction

original state. Restoration efforts by a dedicated preservation group have created an air of optimism to that end.

And finally a few words about the entrepreneurial spirit of the time that made it all possible. Today's parks are for the most part built by huge corporations and conglomerates. This book tries to focus on the adventurous risk-taking of small companies and individuals who put their capital and often their reputations on the line to create something special for the masses. We salute the likes of Benjamin Odell, Fred Ponty, Emanuel Kelmans, Marcus Loew, the Schenck brothers, and others mentioned on these pages. Their vision and daring contributed to making the Hudson Valley such a vibrant location.

Lost Amusement Parks of the Hudson Valley

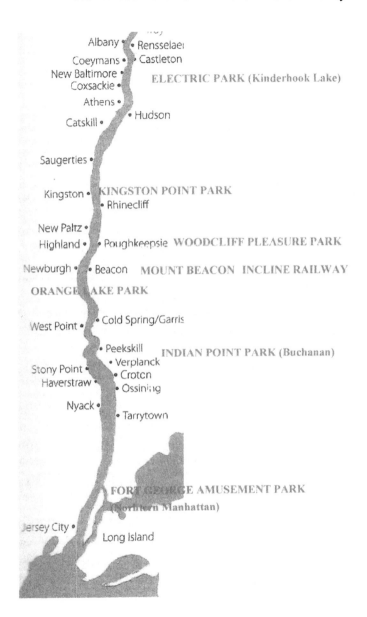

Electric Park

Kinderhook Lake is located in Columbia County, New York and lies about six miles east of the Hudson River. It is equidistant to Albany and Hudson, about 18 miles either way. With an area of approximately one and one half square miles covering 375 acres, it is modest in size. Yet it was the venue for what some have described as "the largest amusement park on the east coast from New York City to Montreal" from its inception in 1901 until its demise sometime during the World War I era. Surrounding the lake are the villages of North Chatham to its northeast and Niverville at its southern border, with the villages of Kinderhook and Valatie further south.

Kinderhook got its name from Henry Hudson. It is believed that on September 18, 1609 Hudson anchored near Stuyvesant Landing just west of what is now Kinderhook. During his several days moored there, he and/or his crew encountered some Native American children who were probably in awe of his ship and the strangely dressed crew. Either then or shortly thereafter Hudson named the land there *Kinderhoek*

Lost Amusement Parks of the Hudson Valley

(Kinderhook). Translated from Dutch, it means "children's corner (or point)".

Kinderhook became a Dutch settlement and was one of the original towns of Columbia County. Today, the Town of Kinderhook is comprised of several villages. Among the town's distinctions, Martin Van Buren, the eighth president of the United States, was born in what is now the village of Kinderhook. He later purchased an estate called *Lindenwald* where he lived for 21 years until his death in 1862. The house left Van Buren ownership when Martin's son John amassed large gambling debts. Shortly after, Jennie Jerome, Winston Churchill's mother, lived in the Van Buren house after it was acquired by her father. Washington Irving also called Kinderhook home while writing *Rip Van Winkle* and gathering material for the enduring *The Legend of Sleepy Hollow*.

A park called Great Park was built along the lake's eastern shore after the Civil War. It provided boating, a pavilion for dancing, a hand-pushed gravity "roller coaster", a restaurant, and refreshment stands which served a special concoction of blood orange juice. After a few decades, the Industrial Revolution and the emergence of electric power started taking hold. The Electric Park at Kinderhook Lake was one of dozens that opened around the country between the late 1890s and the first two decades of the 20th century. They were inspired by a prototype amusement park at the 1893 World Columbian Exposition in Chicago. The first large scale Ferris wheel and a prototype for a modern midway originated there.

The term "electric park" was primarily generic (they also went by the names of "White City parks" and "trolley parks"). It referred to that genre of amusement parks that were developed, owned, and usually operated by railroad companies and power companies. The parks were constructed at an electric trolley stop and were often illuminated by colorful lights.

Electric Park

Electric trolleys rose to popularity in the late 19th century. Two modes developed: The street railway system (or "streetcars") served the needs of a single metropolitan area. But the development of interurban systems which linked towns and cities opened up great opportunities for electric companies and railroad operators (sometimes one in the same).

The rails provided the means for the massive movement of people during the work week. But weekend business was weak and owners bemoaned the fact that cars sat largely idle. Many owners, in an effort to maximize profits, developed destinations for families during the times when people were not at work. Inspired by Europe's very popular "pleasure" parks with their formal gardens, landscaped strolling paths, and picnic areas, owners ran rails to their newly developed parks. It wasn't long, however, before the marriage of power companies, railroads, and "amusement" parks was complete. Visitors soon succumbed to the lure of electric lights and the thrill of amusement rides as they helped fill the trolley cars seven days a week. Soon all horse-drawn trolley lines were replaced by electric power leading to the parks' entrances. "Electric" amusement parks were born.

The Albany & Hudson Railroad Company (in 1909 it reorganized as the Albany Southern and in 1924 as Eastern New York Utilities Corporation) was credited with establishing the first interurban third-rail line in the country. It quickly capitalized on that achievement when it saw opportunity at Kinderhook Lake. In addition, the population between Albany and Hudson along the Hudson Valley was substantial, close to 250,000 by the early 1900s, an impressive total of potential customers. By 1902, just over 1,000,000 people rode the line. By 1905, as the park's popularity grew, that figure grew to 1,353,869 paying customers.

The Electric Park at Kinderhook Lake opened in 1901, owned and operated by the Albany & Hudson Railroad Company. Double tracks were installed to accommodate visitors from Albany. The final switch to electric power was in place by 1900 with the current generated by water power from Stuyvesant Falls. Many attractions and the colorful lights at the park were powered by the same third-rail source as the trolleys. Some nearby homes drew current from the system as well. The owners advertised steadily in 25 newspapers, including those in Rensselaer, Albany, Schenectady, Cohoes, Watervliet, Hudson, Coxsacie, Hudson and Catskill. Billboards were placed in strategic areas. And the people came. One newspaper account reported a crowd of 12,000 on July 4, 1904. Despite the park's impressive attendance figures, the rail line felt that the park was only marginally self-sustaining.

Troy's visitors would link to Albany where they met their connection at Broadway and State Street. They would then set out on their one-hour journey to the lake's east shore at Niverville near the park's entrance. Pleasure seekers from points south such as Hudson and towns along the way flocked to enjoy a day's outing as well. The round-trip excursion fare from Albany and Hudson was 40 forty cents which included admission to the park. Visitors from Schenectady and Saugerties paid 75 cents. Those who arrived by their own device paid ten cents for admission to the park. Local trains left Hudson and Albany mostly on an hourly basis from 6:00 AM until 11:00 PM with one express train each day and a special late evening departure trip as well.

However, questions of the railroad's safety tempered the park's successful opening in 1901. On May 26, 1901 two electric cars racing at 40 miles per hour in opposite directions hoping to catch an open switch, collided just outside of Greenbush. The passengers were returning from a day's merriment at Electric Park. The wreckage took the lives of five people (including both motormen) and injured scores of others. Another tragic trolley crash in August 1902 resulted in the deaths of a five year old boy and a 20 year old woman on their way to Electric Park. Apparently the cars were running to the park at excessive speeds on a particularly busy weekend.

Electric Park

It should be noted that Kinderhook's Electric Park debuted some two years even before entrepreneurs Frederick Thompson and Elmer Dundy opened the historic Luna Park at Coney Island on May 16, 1903. At its peak, Luna Park's 1,000,000 lights lit up the night sky. Its wild popularity spurred amusement developer Frederick Ingersoll to create 44 other Luna Parks by 1914, not only in the United States but around the world. Today, many European countries still refer to their amusement parks as "luna parks".

Though the Electric Park at Kinderhook Lake was already up and running, the success of Ingersoll's parks and Coney Island enticed a number of American cities to create electric parks of their own. Some cities hosted two or more of these parks during this period of expansion and the competition between them could be fierce. The weaker ones did not survive very long. By the time of Ingersoll's death in 1927, many had already disappeared. The Electric Park at Kinderhook Lake had no nearby competitors but its demise could be attributed to other factors which will be mentioned later.

Electric Park included almost 40 acres of property along the lake's shore line. There is no doubt that the owners' goal (in addition to making a profit) was to create a wholesome entertainment experience for families. Among their stated claims was that Electric Park was "...a place where ladies and children can go unattended". Management took measures to insure a climate of safety, cleanliness, and comfort for guests. Rowdiness was not tolerated. The park was "dry" although, as we'll see later, many male visitors found an avenue to quench their thirsts. The relatively early closing times of 10:30 PM on weekdays and 7:30 PM on Sundays (except for the dance pavilion and theater events) were designed to prevent any trouble. Even the vaudeville company which performed at the park's theater was required to spell out the specifics of their acts in a contract beforehand. This park requirement was designed to avoid any racy or otherwise objectionable material.

Lost Amusement Parks of the Hudson Valley

Adults and children alike were able to enjoy the shows. The park's overall appearance was of paramount importance to its owners.

The park's grand array of rides and activities provided something for everyone. After making their way from the trolley station towards the entrance, visitors were greeted by a large steam-powered Ferris wheel. The sheer size and weight of the attraction made it too cumbersome to move it uphill through the entrance gate. For those so inclined, the ride cost a nickel on top of the trolley/admission fare. A second, electrically-powered Ferris wheel operated inside the park's gates and cost five cents to ride. Like most of the attractions, it was owned and operated by the Albany & Hudson Railroad Company.

A beautiful electric-powered carousel was erected on an island in the lagoon and a bridge was constructed to connect it to the midway. Earlier, during the winter of 1900 and 1901, a bridge was built from the park to Hawley Point where the grand Point Hotel and its saloon were located. The Point served Dobler beer. The bridge was financed by the Dobler Beer Company knowing full well that as more patrons crossed that bridge, the more its pockets would be lined. The wooden bridge was rickety and became a thrill ride in itself. Winds from a severe storm blew the bridge down in April 1911 and it was never rebuilt. Since its pilings were never set in concrete, the loss probably came as no surprise. Subsequent to the collapse, visitors had to rely on horse and buggy to ride around the perimeter of the lake to get to the Point. The Point Hotel burned to the ground in 1912.

The park's roller coaster was also built over the lake around 1907. It was constructed during the winter months so holes needed to be chopped through the ice in order to set its pilings. The ride cost a dime. Of course the standard penny arcade and popular "shoot-the-chutes" (a refreshing precursor to today's water flume rides) were early attractions. For little ones, there was a menagerie to keep them diverted. Animal rides featuring goats, donkeys, and ponies were offered. A miniature

Electric Park

railroad railway was constructed for their enjoyment. Fish from Kinderhook Lake could be observed in an aquarium.

Being on a lake presented plenty of activities. Boats were available for lake navigation at Favour's Beach and at Winslow's boat launch, among other locations. Rowboats could be rented by the hour, day or week. One trip around the lake cost the customer a nickel. For those less energetic there were bathing (with suit rentals) and fishing areas that offered pleasant diversions on a hot summer's day. Tent platforms were erected for families who needed a respite from the excitement.

The European "pleasure garden" influence was evident as well. Beautifully landscaped walkways, flower gardens, and picnic areas were available to all. For those who did not pack their own lunches, there were refreshment stands and a large restaurant. A bowling alley was situated adjacent to the restaurant. The eateries were perhaps the only enterprises not operated by the owners; they were run as private concessions.

The open-air Rustic Theatre brought throngs together twice a day for live entertainment. The seats were built on a slope in tiers down toward the stage, offering superior sight lines. Eventually a canopy was added to shield the 400 patrons from the broiling sun or showers. Early on, operas were held but they were soon supplanted by the more popular vaudeville shows featuring music and slapstick comedy. A reserved seat cost a dime. Shows were held daily at 3:00 PM and 8:30 PM except on Sundays. On the Sabbath, the theater featured "sacred" concerts with a 25-piece orchestra. Ironically, some of the orchestra members were the vaudeville show musicians moonlighting for an extra day's pay. The theater could also be leased by large groups for meetings and lectures. Occasionally, as they gained popularity, movies were increasingly shown.

The dance pavilion's floor measured 130 by 80 feet, making it one of the largest in the state. It became a popular attraction as well by offering afternoon and evening sessions. A separate pavilion housed large church and fellowship gatherings on a reservation basis. The colorfully-attired "Professor Speedy" (in reality 15 year old F. Marvin Callan) performed daring feats from a high dive platform. He performed his comedic plunges into the lake three times daily accompanied by much drama and fanfare. Another high-stake "drama" was the parachute jumper who lifted off in a hot air balloon then parachuted down hopefully within the sight of park patrons. Stories of the balloon being blown off course and landing on the roofs of disgruntled neighbors were not uncommon.

Though the park was situated on a "dry" portion of Columbia County (Chatham Township), shrewd entrepreneurs skirted around this obstacle by establishing drinking establishments on its outskirts where imbibing was legal. Numerous saloons were built in and around the lake to satisfy patrons who desired to imbibe. The most prominent were Cap Shaver's, Mulligan's, the Fisherman's Rest, and the Point.

Adam (Cap) Shaver's establishment was built on a small island on the west side of the lake in 1904. The two story structure took up almost all the space. With a full galley and ten bedrooms upstairs in addition to the bar, it efficiently utilized the space allotted. The venue also employed a piano player to keep the gents happy. Men who wished to take leave of their families for a respite would, in the day's vernacular, head to a "rest area" or go "fishing for beer". Cap Shaver's closed in 1916. The nearby Fishermen's Rest was located on the aptly named "One Tree" Island.

As locals remember it, men would rent boats and paddle out or walk across the bridge to the area's most popular saloon located at Hawley Point. The Point Hotel's bar was huge and was kept very busy during peak season. It employed a staff of 60 bartenders and waiters on special occasions such as the Fourth of July celebrations and the Farmers' Picnic in August. The Farmers' Picnic was the big social event of the summer for farmers and their families. Lunch spreads were set out under the trees while orators spoke of farm prices, politics, and plans for the Chatham

Electric Park

Fair, just one month away. Wives shared recipes and listened to each others' tales of child rearing. As the day wore on into evening, the men gather at the Point's bar. The "men's only" mahogany bar was kept busy as guests pontificated further on local and national affairs. Boisterous singalongs and impromptu horse races frequently ensued. The Point Hotel burned somewhere between 1912 and 1914. Three bars were still running in 1916 but it is believed they were shuttered shortly after as the United States entered the war.

In addition to the Point Hotel, for two dollars one could stay in nearby Valatie at the U.S. Hotel which featured "modern" amenities such as hot and cold running water and electric lights. The building still stands.

Electric Park thrived and was a beehive of activity during the warm months. However, the park was not exactly dormant during the cold and snow season. Bundled-up adventurers could take a toboggan ride down the snow-covered "shoot-the-chutes" ramp. The ride was much longer during the winter as the rider would skip along the ice until friction took over. Ice skating became popular on the lake. Curling enthusiasts held competitions. The dance pavillon was kept open for those interested in more tranquil and warmer forms of entertainment. Ice was harvested from the lake to be stored until the next tourist season rolled around.

But the good times were not to last forever. Electric parks had a good run but by the end of the second decade of the 20th century their numbers were declining. The onset of World War I in 1914 shook the world. By 1917, the United States felt it could no longer maintain its neutrality and began sending troops and arms abroad to support its allies. The war had a great impact on the country. The mood had changed. Many families were without their breadwinners. Austerity had taken hold. Expendable income was reduced. Prohibition was looming and the saloon business was on its way out.

But more importantly in the case of electric parks, automobile travel was gaining popularity. Those fortunate enough to own cars now had more options open to them and were not restricted to rail line locations. The golden age of trolleys, the core of the electric park's existence, was starting to fade away. Some of the electric parks, their largest attractions built from wood, succumbed to fire. A new form of entertainment, the radio, kept many people in their own homes as an alternative to traveling. Huddling around a radio listening to what are now classics was economical as well as entertaining. Local silent film theaters were springing up. State parks were now a choice for many as well. And this was all happening well before The Great Stock Market Crash of October 1929 and the ensuing Great Depression.

There is debate over when the Electric Park at Kinderhook Lake ultimately closed. There is speculation that it closed around Labor Day 1916 in the war years. The dance pavilion burned in 1916 only to be replaced a short time later. The replacement collapsed in 1920 under the weight of heavy snow a few years later. The park may have attempted to reopen a year or two later but the end was inevitable. Some conjecture has it that the park may have lingered into 1920 or 1921 on a limited basis but there is no documentation to substantiate that claim. Additional industry-wide pressures such as increasing costs of upgrades, insurance, and general upkeep may have hastened the demise. Dates aside, the Electric Park at Kinderhook, once described by its owners as "all that is best in refined amusements" could not overcome all of these influences. Sadly, the last trolley to the park rolled in on December 21, 1919, though the park may have struggled along for a year or two more.

Once abandoned, the park became an unofficial playground for trespassing youngsters who enjoyed climbing the coaster's framework, exploring the carousel looking for souvenirs, and racing across the bridge. Some of the attractions were sold to other parks that were still managing to hang on. Others were sold to new parks being created, but those would now be built away from trolley lines. The larger wooden rides were dismantled. It is believed some of the local homes were benefactors of the lumber. The Eaton Wrecking Company dismantled the roller coaster around 1920 and took the lumber as remuneration. The carousel was shipped to Columbus, Ohio in 1922. The railroad station burned in 1928. In that same year the Rustic Theatre also burned, a somber final act for a venue that had entertained tens of thousands for a generation. The last major remnants of the park were now gone.

    Little remains of this once idyllic park. The trolley routes leading to the park are only partially navigable. One vivid reminder of its glorious past is a street sign located on Route 203 as one approaches the lake. It reads "Electric Park Road". A more poignant observation can be made as one surveys the lake. A few of the carousel's pilings may be observed today when lake levels are low. Several of the grand roller coaster's vertical support beams cling to life just above the lake's surface, slowly rotting from the elements. Driving along Electric Park Road, if one looks to the left just past the lagoon which housed the carousel, a stone entrance which led to the bowling alley and restaurant still stands. A century ago, parents with their wide-eyed children in tow would walk through the archway to an adventure that created unforgettable memories.

Lost Amusement Parks of the Hudson Valley

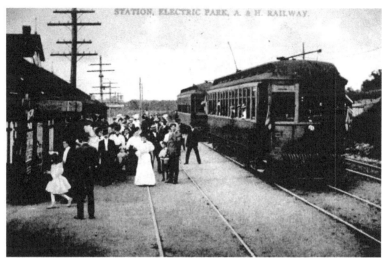

The Albany and Hudson Railway Company operated trolleys to Electric Park. They also owned and operated the park. Shown here are visitors departing the cars readying for a day's outing. Double cars, such as the ones seen here, ran on weekends to accommodate the large crowds. Single cars ran most other times. *Courtesy of the Columbia County Historical Society, the Robert and Evelyn Monthie Slide Collection.*

Railway workers pose in front of the Electric Park station. Note the cow catcher in the front of the #20 car. *Courtesy of the Columbia County Historical Society, the Robert and Evelyn Monthie Slide Collection*

Electric Park

With the depot in the background, arriving patrons walk along beautifully manicured paths. The owners often stressed that the park's safety, cleanliness, and beautiful landscaping were what brought people back for return visits in addition to the rides and other attractions. *Courtesy of the Columbia County Historical Society, the Robert and Evelyn Monthie Slide Collection.*

Lost Amusement Parks of the Hudson Valley

Groups attending Electric Park were offered special combination tickets. The Ancient City Lodge, Number 452, received a package which included round trip trolley transportation from Albany, a luncheon, and a reserved seat to a performance at the Rustic Theatre. Groups could also reserve a pavilion for the day. The Green Island Methodist Church group took a boat from Troy operated by the Albany and Troy Steamboat Company. At day's end they could return via trolley or boat. Children under 12 year of age received a discount. The ticket

Electric Park

Entrance Walk, Electric Park, Hudson, N.Y.

This postcard shows the path leading to the park's entrance with Kinderhook Lake to the left. The park maintained relatively early closing hours in its early years to prevent any rowdiness so as to reinforce its family oriented reputation. However, the dance pavilion stayed open until midnight. *Courtesy of Larry Laliberte.*

ALBANY & HUDSON R. R. CO., OWNERS

OUR PATRONS

Electric Park is a place of refinement for people of refinement.

Ladies and children unattended by escorts may visit the Park at either afternoon or evening performance without fear of annoyance from any source.

The patrons of the Park will confer a favor upon the management by reporting to the manager, the slightest inattention of incivility upon the part of any employee.

Writing desk, telegraph blanks, time tables on all railroads can be had at the Park Treasurer's Office at entrance.

Parcels, wraps, etc., can be checked at the Check Room in end of Restaurant Building for five cents.

No intoxicating liquors sold or allowed on the grounds.

Swings, etc., can be found in the grove, for the use of the children.

Don't start to rush for the Station when the last act is half on. It is bad manners and besides the Station Gates will not be opened until the curtain falls.

Ladies wearing large hats in the reserved seats will remember those in the rear.

No smoking allowed in the theatre.

NOTICE.—All persons occupying reserved seats must have tickets.

Mothers with children should not try to be the first on the cars at the Station. There is always cars enough to take all home.

DANCING IN LAKE PAVILION

Every Week Day—after each performance. Afternoons, 5 to 8. Evenings, 10 to 12. Saturdays, 2 to 6, 10 to 12. Full Orchestra

DAILY CONCERTS

By Gartland's Orchestra—2 to 3 and 7 to 8 p. m.

CASINO RESTAURANT

The owners reminded visitors about proper etiquette while stressing that the park was a place of "refinement". The park was "dry" hence the statement about intoxicating beverages. Those wishing to imbibe made their way to one of several "wet" areas on the lake. *Courtesy of the Columbia County Historical Society, the Robert and Evelyn Monthie Slide Collection.*

Electric Park

Visitors, in their splendid attire, stroll along the crowded midway. Note the plants along the roofline on the left. The midway offered shooting galleries, a penny arcade, refreshments, and places to purchase souvenirs (often postcards). *Courtesy of the Columbia County Historical Society, the Robert and Evelyn Monthie Slide Collection.*

Boaters enjoy some quiet time on the lake. There were many boat houses along the lake where visitors could rent boats (one of these boat houses can be seen along the shore to the left). The main amusement area can be seen in the background with the roller coaster looming over all. *Courtesy of Larry Laliberte.*

Lost Amusement Parks of the Hudson Valley

With the boats for hire in the foreground, the carousel (often spelled "carousal" in the day) sits in the lagoon. A lovely walking bridge was built from the shore to the carousel. Next to the carousel was a refreshment stand that featured homemade ice cream. *Courtesy of the Columbia County Historical Society, the Robert and Evelyn Monthie Slide Collection.*

Electric Park had many peaceful places where folks could get away from the midway and the attractions. One could pull up a boat on the shore and take a leisurely walk along the lake. There were secluded picnic areas, flower gardens, and lovely wooded paths (one was dubbed "Lover's Lane"). *Courtesy of the Columbia County Historical Society, the Robert and Evelyn Monthie Slide Collection.*

Electric Park

The crews at these two boat docks were kept busy by fishermen and those who just wanted to glide on the lake. Many men, wishing to take leave of their families for a spell to go "fishing for beer", would navigate to the "wet" area of the lake. Boats could be rented by the hour, day, or week. An excursion around the lake by motor boat cost a nickel per person. The lake was well stocked to the delight of the fishermen. *Courtesy of the Columbia County Historical Society, the Robert and Evelyn Monthie Slide Collection.*

This photograph, taken in August 1907, shows a group floating about in their Adirondack styled boat. Off to the right, on a tiny treed island, stood "Cap" Shaver's Island. In 1904, Cap Shaver (Adam Shaver) built a two-story structure that covered most of the 150 by 30 foot island. Built in the "wet" area of the lake, it had a dock to receive male patrons and to launch them (in various states of inebriation) back to the midway area. He catered to men who were looking for a "rest area" away from their families. Once there, gents could imbibe to their heart's content and eat some home made grub from the full galley. To the left of the picture is "One Tree" Island, home to the Fishermen's Rest, another drinking establishment. As the war intensified, interest in the park waned and the drinking establishments soon vanished. *Courtesy of the Columbia County Historical Society, the Robert and Evelyn Monthie Slide Collection.*

Electric Park

Carousels were integral parts to all amusement parks at the turn of the century. The calliopes rang out their unmistakable sounds as beautifully sculptured wooden chariots and animals (some gracefully "jumping" through the air) spun around to the delight of young and old. The image above shows the path leading to Electric Park's carousel. It was actually a bridge that crossed the lagoon to where the carousel was housed. On the left is a refreshment stand which offered ice cream sodas for a nickel. The posed image (below) gives a feel not only for some of the carousel's details but of the clothing finery of the day. Electric Park's carousel was built by William Mongals, a legendary figure in amusement designs. Its band organ was manufactured in Waldkirch, Germany. The carousel was powered by 600 volts of electricity, just like the Ferris wheel located inside the park (the other Ferris wheel, located outside of the entrance, was steam-powered).
Above image from the author's collection, . on; image below courtesy of the Columbia County Historical Society, the Robert and Evelyn Monthie Slide Collection.

Lost Amusement Parks of the Hudson Valley

Both the carousel and the roller coaster were built out in a lagoon. The carousel house, foreground, was simply abandoned after the park closed. For about six years, it was visited by vagrants and teenagers. One teenager told a tale of visiting the carousel one day, looking for mementos, when he was half frightened to death by a man who had decided to use it as a temporary home. In 1922, the carousel was shipped to Columbus, Ohio where it was refurbished and used in another amusement park. *Courtesy of Larry Laliberte.*

Most electric parks featured dance halls or pavilions. The Electric Park at Kinderhook Lake was no exception. Its dance pavilion was one of the largest in New York State. Accompanying music was often provided by Stella's Star Orchestra. *Courtesy of the Columbia County Historical Society, the Robert and Evelyn Monthie Slide Collection.*

Electric Park

Lost Amusement Parks of the Hudson Valley

The park had two Ferris wheels, one located inside the gates and one just outside the entrance. The steam-powered wheel was left outside since the owners found it too heavy and bulky to move up the hill in to the park proper. The ride cost a nickel. The electrically powered wheel was located inside the park. It too cost a nickel extra. Notice the barrels covered by a small canopy. They were set out by the park's owners and contained drinking water for customers. The neighboring concessionaire, realizing he was losing customers if they drank the free water, placed a rusty cup, it is told, inside the top barrel which prompted many to sidle up to his stand and purchase a sanitary beverage. In another equally devious move, he was known to surreptitiously drain the barrels of their water. One of the young men who operated the Ferris wheel was prone to halting the ride when an attractive young lady reached the very top. After showing some degree of distress, she was finally lowered to the ground where the overly attentive ride operator provided tender comfort. *Courtesy of Larry Laliberte.*

Electric Park

The "Golden Age" of amusement parks is considered to be roughly 1900 through the 1920s. The mere proliferation of parks may have led to that designation but more advanced thrill rides contributed to their popularity as well. Roller coasters were being built higher and faster with each new park. The coaster at Kinderhook Lake was fairly large for its time (built in 1907). These two postcard images were taken from almost identical spots. The carousel house is seen on the right. Men and women often traveled in separate groups during this time. *Above image courtesy of Larry Laliberte; image below courtesy of the Columbia County Historical Society, the Robert and Evelyn Monthie Slide Collection.*

Lost Amusement Parks of the Hudson Valley

This group poses in front of the roller coaster. The penny scale to the left was another amusement park staple. In 1920, several years after the park closed, the coaster was dismantled and the salvaged wood was used to construct homes. *Courtesy of the Columbia County Historical Society, the Robert and Evelyn Monthie Slide Collection.*

The park's "shoot-the-chutes" was not unlike many others of the day. What made it somewhat different is that it was used as a toboggan run in the winter. *Courtesy of Larry Laliberte.*

Electric Park

The Electric Park at Kinderhook became somewhat of a park for all seasons. Pictured here is the winter version of "shoot-the chutes". The ride was eventually expanded to three chutes. The toboggans landed on the frozen lake which extended the ride a lot further than the summer version. The park's promotion of the toboggan run stated "Those who have tried the slide know that it is not dangerous and it is one of the greatest sports ever indulged in". Ice skaters could glide the lake accompanied by an "electric orchestrion" (a mechanical organ). The dance pavilion remained open in the winter every Wednesday and Saturday evening from 8 PM until midnight. On other nights, the pavilion hosted euchre clubs and private parties. Curling events were held as well. *Courtesy of the Columbia County Historical Society, the Robert and Evelyn Monthie Slide Collection.*

If the amusements weren't enough to entertain youngsters, they had plenty of room to run in the playground in this glen. It is surprising to see glass backboards for the basketball court. Most were wooden around this time. Pony rides were available here too. *Courtesy of the Columbia County Historical Society, the Robert and Evelyn Monthie Slide Collection.*

The "pony track" entertained young and old alike. *Courtesy of Larry Laliberte.*

Electric Park

There were a number of areas to swim at Kinderhook Lake. Bathing suits could be rented. The high dive platform pictured in this photograph was available to all bathers. However, when "Professor" Speedy performed his act three times daily, the diving board was raised to its maximum height. *Courtesy of the Columbia County Historical Society, the Robert and Evelyn Monthie Slide Collection.*

The pavilion shown here provided a respite and some shade. It was a good place to bring a picnic lunch. The pavilion could be leased for the day and it was a popular venue with civic and church groups. *Courtesy of the Columbia County Historical Society, the Robert and Evelyn Monthie Slide Collection.*

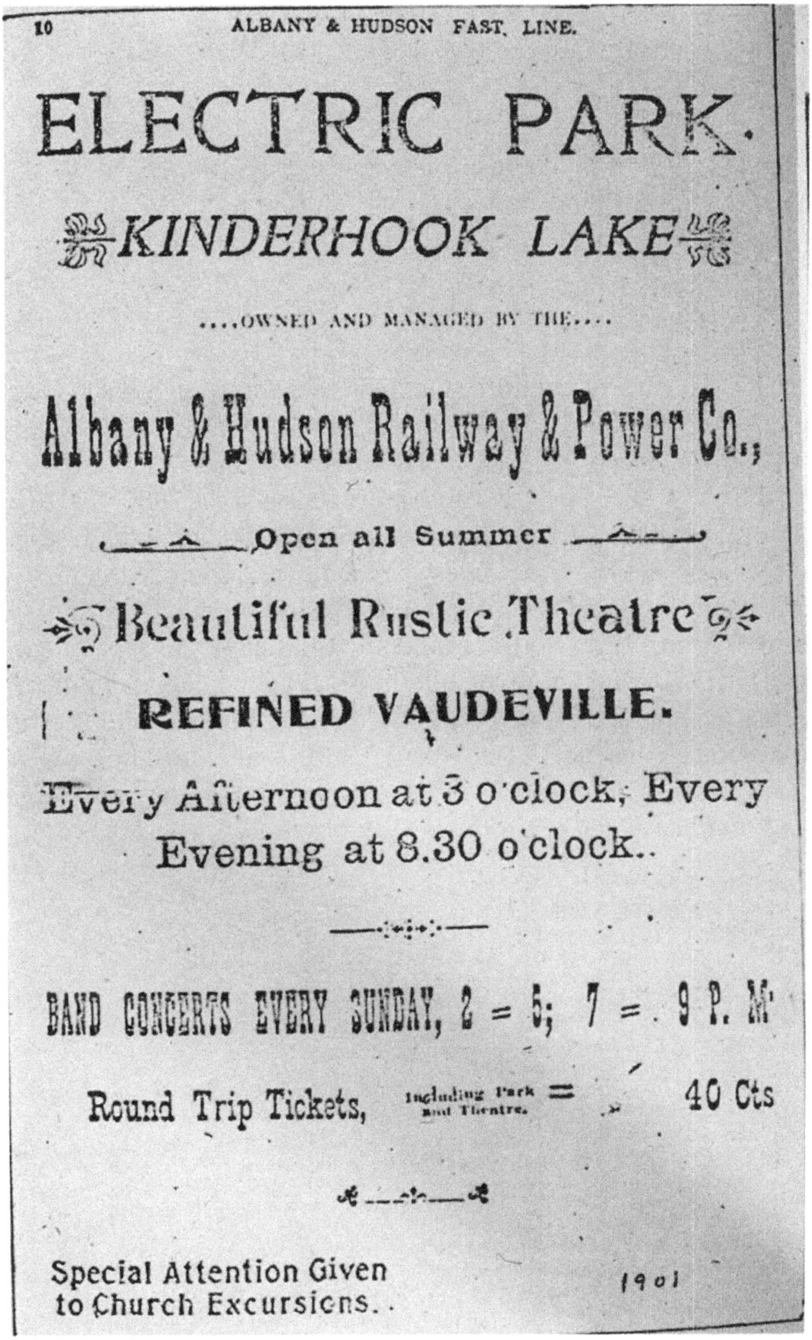

ELECTRIC PARK.

KINDERHOOK LAKE

....OWNED AND MANAGED BY THE....

Albany & Hudson Railway & Power Co.,

Open all Summer

Beautiful Rustic Theatre

REFINED VAUDEVILLE.

Every Afternoon at 3 o'clock, Every Evening at 8.30 o'clock.

BAND CONCERTS EVERY SUNDAY, 2 = 5; 7 = 9 P. M.

Round Trip Tickets, Including Park and Theatre = 40 Cts

Special Attention Given to Church Excursions.

1901

Albany & Hudson Fast Line.

Electric Park

The Rustic Theatre entertained hundreds of people each day. Originally, operettas were the bill of fare until the park's owners realized the public wanted more variety that would appeal to all ages. Instead, "refined" vaudeville shows became the staple presentations. In 1901, for 40 cents, a patron received round-trip trolley fair, park admission, and a reserved seat to the theater. Acts changed every Thursday and included quite a variety of performers including Montague's Cockatoo (spelled "cukatoo" in the program) Circus, the Reiff Brothers- America's greatest singing and dancing act, Bryant and Saville-musical comedians, Eddie Horan-comedian, Knapp and Knapp-the "Swede" and his girl, and McCune and Grant-a comedy bar act. The Rustic Theatre also hosted movie nights. *Courtesy of the Columbia County Historical Society, the Robert and Evelyn Monthie Slide Collection.*

Lost Amusement Parks of the Hudson Valley

This photograph was taken from the top of the stands looking toward the stage of the Rustic Theatre. The buildings on either side served as the "wings" and dressing rooms. Note that the piano, always part of a good vaudeville show, is located on the right side of the stage. The hill's natural terrain provided the element for perfect sight lines to the stage. Pictures on this page *courtesy of the Columbia County Historical Society, the Robert and Evelyn Monthie Slide Collection.*

This looks like a sold-out show at the 400 seat theater. By this time, a roof had been added to protect patrons from the elements. Posted bills reminded the audience about proper etiquette. For example, ladies were asked to remove large hats and it was considered poor manners to leave before the show concluded.

Electric Park

A lavish set was constructed for this production at the Rustic Theatre. In addition to vaudeville, special shows were produced as well. One of the last plays held at the Rustic was on Labor Day of 1912. It was a three act play called "Wife in Name Only". *Courtesy of the Columbia County Historical Society, the Robert and Evelyn Monthie Slide Collection.*

Parrotville Steamer Company responding to an alarm.   Electric Park, season of 1905

The caption on this 1905 photograph is self explanatory. Montague's Cockatoo Circus also featured chariot races. *Courtesy of the Columbia County Historical Society, the Robert and Evelyn Monthie Slide Collection.*

Refreshment stands abounded at Electric Park. The most popular items seemed to be Cracker Jacks, peanuts, ice cream, candy (chocolates), and "blood" orange juice. Some stands kept their blood orange juice ingredients a secret. One stand's Cracker Jacks slogan was "...can't be beat by anything made to eat". It is interesting to note that none of the stands served hot dogs. Hot dogs were just beginning to gain popularity at entertainment venues around the turn of the century. The famous Nathan's at Coney Island didn't start serving its product until 1916. *Courtesy of the Columbia County Historical Society, the Robert and Evelyn Monthie Slide Collection.*

Electric Park

In this circa 1916 image, shortly before the park's demise, this combination pharmacy, waiting room, bakery, and lunch spot was built near the entrance. When the park folded, the store continued to function. It is not know when it ceased to operate. Close scrutiny reveals that the sale of hot frankfurters had finally arrived. *Courtesy of Larry Laliberte.*
In this circa 1916 image, shortly before the park's demise, this combination pharmacy, waiting room, bakery, and lunch spot was built near the entrance. When the park folded, the store continued to function. It is not know when it ceased to operate. Close scrutiny reveals that the sale of hot frankfurters had finally arrived. *Courtesy of Larry Laliberte.*

Visitors pose by the Point Hotel at Hawley Point. The venue was perhaps the busiest of all the hotels and bars in the vicinity. After the walking bridge to the Point collapsed, Electric Park visitors needed to use horse and buggy or, if they were fortunate enough, automobile to drive the lake's perimeter to the nice location. *Courtesy of the Columbia County Historical Society, the Robert and Evelyn Monthie Slide Collection.*

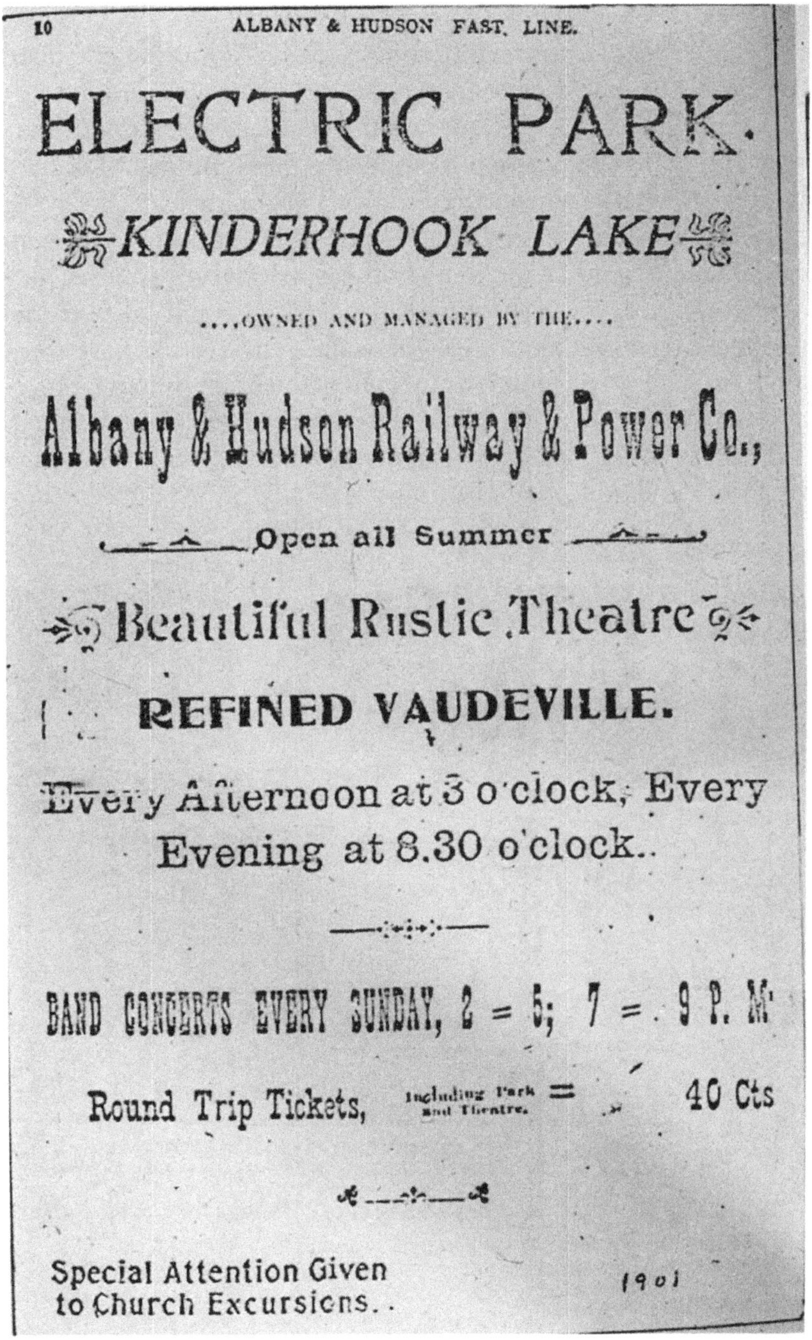

10 ALBANY & HUDSON FAST LINE.

ELECTRIC PARK.

KINDERHOOK LAKE

....OWNED AND MANAGED BY THE....

Albany & Hudson Railway & Power Co.,

Open all Summer

Beautiful Rustic Theatre

REFINED VAUDEVILLE.

Every Afternoon at 3 o'clock, Every Evening at 8.30 o'clock.

BAND CONCERTS EVERY SUNDAY, 2 = 5; 7 = 9 P. M.

Round Trip Tickets, Including Park and Theatre = 40 Cts

1901

Special Attention Given to Church Excursions.

Electric Park

In this circa 1901 advertisement (above) for the Point Hotel, superlatives abound. Its bar attracted more than its share of patrons, particularly during special events like the 4th of July or the Farmers' Picnic. In the image below, visitors are ready to embark on the three minute walk across the bridge from Hawley Point to the Electric Park midway. The bridge was constructed during the winter of 1900 and 1901. Pilings were sunk after holes were chopped in the ice. The bridge apparently was never too sturdy as the pilings were never set in concrete. Men would take advantage of that weakness by adding a thrill to the walk. They would purposely shake the bridge causing their female companions to shriek in mock horror. The bridge collapsed in April of 1911. The Point Hotel burned about a year later. *Courtesy of the Columbia County Historical Society, the Robert and Evelyn Monthie Slide Collection.*

Lost Amusement Parks of the Hudson Valley

After the park's demise, the lake became a tranquil place once again. This photograph of Electric Park Village was taken in the 1920s. *Courtesy of the Columbia County Historical Society, the Robert and Evelyn Monthie Slide Collection.*

One of the few reminders of Electric's Park heyday is this street sign. The road leads to the lake's east shore where most of the activity took place. *Photograph by Wes Gottlock.*

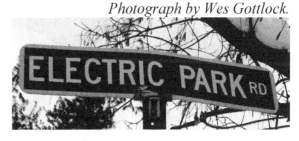

It is believed this stone arch led to the bowling alley and restaurant near the park's entrance. It now fronts a private residence. Countless people must have walked through this passage with wonder and excitement anticipating a beautiful day in this once glorious park. *Photograph by Wes Gottlock.*

Woodcliff Pleasure Park

The Woodcliff Pleasure Park in Poughkeepsie occupied a site that is now the northernmost portion of the Marist College campus, encompassing the present-day athletic field and a student residential housing complex just off the east bank of the Hudson River. It covered 27 acres. It was a premier park whose quick rise and sudden demise were nothing short of startling. The park's heyday spanned the years from 1927 until 1941 but little of its unique history has been preserved. It is worth examining some of the site's past which led to the park's establishment. The contrasting transformation from a bucolic estate to a full service amusement park in a year's time is extraordinary.

John Flack Winslow was born in 1810 in Bennington, Vermont. He worked in the iron industry along with his partner Erastus Corning. Together they owned the Rensselaer Iron Works and the Albany Iron Works. These companies were among the foremost producers of iron in the country.

In 1861 John Winslow and another partner, John A. Griswold, began working with Captain John Ericsson on the production of the ironclad warship *Monitor*. After trying to get the Naval Board to act on their plan they met with President Abraham Lincoln. Lincoln was excited by the idea and chaired a meeting between Winslow, Griswold, the Naval Board, the Secretary of the Navy, and many influential navy officers. The Naval Board supported the idea but was slow to act; therefore Winslow financed the cost of building the ship largely by himself. During the battle of Hampton Roads, Virginia over March 8–9, 1862 the Confederacy tried to break the Union's naval blockade of international trade going to Norfolk and Richmond. The *Monitor* was so successful against the *Merrimac* that the government ordered more ironclads. By 1863 Winslow and Griswold had produced 35 ironclads using the same design as the original *Monitor*. These warships patrolled the east coast of the United States during the Civil War.

In 1867 John Winslow married his second wife, Harriet Wickes of Poughkeepsie. Together they raised two children. John served as the president of Rensselaer Polytechnic Institute in Troy for three years before retiring in 1868. When John retired, he and his family moved to an estate on Hyde Park Road in Poughkeepsie, New York. The Winslows called the estate Wood Cliff (the amusement park always connected the words and a variant spelling of *Woodcliffe* was occasionally observed in print).

The main house was made of brick when John bought it. Major renovations were done. Among them, the exterior of the main residence was sealed in clapboard to make the house look more Victorian. The residence included 35 rooms and a 150 foot tall watchtower. The estate also contained three summer houses: *Crag, Cliff,* and *Lookout.* They were situated on a lovely wooded property overlooking the Hudson River. *Cliff* needed to be rebuilt several times due to fires. *Cliff's* close proximity to the railroad below allowed spewing cinders to ignite it. The estate had greenhouses, a farm, many winding paths, foot bridges, and a small stream flowing through it. A small island in the middle of the stream was shaped like the *Monitor.*

The estate was considered to be one of the finest along the Hudson's banks. When John died in 1893 his family continued to live at Wood Cliff. On April 22, 1926, shortly after his second wife Harriet Wickes Winslow died, the estate was sold to John B. and Elizabeth Marion.

The Winslow descendants felt secure in the knowledge that the Marions would continue to care for their beloved estate. But about eight months later, the Marions' focus changed. They received an offer from Fred Ponty of Rye (also Port Chester), New York who wished to turn the 27-acre estate into an amusement park (or "pleasure" park as they were often known). A deal was struck and Ponty purchased the property with all of the extant structures from John B. and Elizabeth Marion on December 31, 1926. The deed was recorded on April 18, 1927.

Ponty was a real estate developer and entrepreneur who had experience in such ventures. Around 1921 Ponty, along with a partner named Joseph Haight, built Paradise Park in Rye, New York on the grounds where Rye Playland still stands today. It was much larger than its competitor, the Rye Beach Pleasure Park. Nevertheless, Ponty's operation was considered honky-tonk. The park became rife with rowdiness, pickpockets, unsanitary conditions, and run-down shacks. Paradise Park never fully recovered from a large fire in 1926. Soon after, Ponty was bought out to make way for the now historic Rye Playland which opened its gates in May 1928 and to this day remains the only government-owned and operated amusement park in the United States.

Ponty then set his sights on creating his dream, the Woodcliff Pleasure Park. The location was ideal. Bordering the Hudson River's east bank, there was ample dock space for day liners from New York City. The liners transported as many as 18,000 weekend day trippers up the Hudson stopping at various locations during the park's prime. Several thousand of those spent their time at Woodcliff. In addition, trolley service would transport local fun seekers from downtown Poughkeepsie. Ample parking (across what is now Route 9 where Home Depot now stands would be available to those fortunate enough to own cars. On June 9, 1927 Ponty petitioned the town of

Woodcliff Pleasure Park

Poughkeepsie for a license to open his dream park although there is evidence that the park opened before final approval. The Woodcliff Pleasure Park, sometimes referred to as "the finest in the East" and "Coney Island without the sand" (although Ponty would later add sand to the shore to create a "beach") was a reality.

While *Ain't She Sweet* topped the music charts in June 1927, the park opened despite some conjecture that it officially debuted in 1928. Several accounts support this fact. Newspaper accounts declared the official opening date as June 20, 1927. The announcement highlighted the Blue Streak roller coaster and a 110 by 54 foot outdoor ballroom, the largest in the state. But there is evidence it may have opened a bit earlier. There exists a newspaper account of an assault on a patron by park employees at the Woodcliff Pleasure Park on June 12, 1927. Two park employees were arrested after the incident. A *Popular Science Magazine* article from August 1927 reported that the Blue Streak roller coaster was up and running. A baseball tournament was held that year as well. It's possible the park opened on a limited basis in 1927 and didn't reach full operation until 1928.

Ponty invested over $1,000,000 in his park. Most of the Winslow estate structures remained. Some were retrofitted for park use, including the North Lodge. The Winslow mansion, with its beautiful mahogany woodwork and elegant stairway, became an inn. The gate houses became entrance points. But the stables and the stableman's house were torn down. The ornate pink ticket house right off Albany Post Road became a highly recognizable landmark. Ponty preserved as many groves as possible and took measures to replant many of the shrubs and small trees he had to remove. When all was said and done, the park would provide an incredible variety of entertainment.

Bumper cars, pony rides, carousels, a tunnel of love, Ferris wheels, arcades, a giant airplane swing, midway games, "shoot-the-chutes" also called "chute-the-chutes, shooting galleries, whips, and lake boat rides were on the park's menu of attractions. A Caterpillar ride was added. This low coaster would snake around and occasionally envelop its victims in a dark cocoon-like covering eliciting joyful shrieks of fright and horror.

In addition to these standard fare midway attractions and the huge dance hall, wrestling and boxing matches were held periodically. A roller skating rink was built. A challenging Tom Thumb golf course came along. Fireworks displays often lit up the night sky. Traveling circuses made their way to Woodcliff. The Ringling Brothers Barnum and Bailey Circus was a special attraction. Special events were held such as in the August 1930 extravaganza to celebrate the opening of the Poughkeepsie/Highland Bridge (now the Mid-Hudson Bridge). There was a field for exhibition baseball games and equestrian events. The grounds included lovely gardens and secluded picnic areas for those seeking respite from the midways. The groves and paths were colorfully illuminated during the evening hours. The lovely inn housed a restaurant, a dance hall (and later an outside dance area as well), and a bar. Dances were usually accompanied by live orchestras.

But two things set the Woodcliff Pleasure Park apart from its contemporaries. It was the home of the Blue Streak roller coaster and one of the largest swimming pools in the country. The Blue Streak was built over a ten acre apple and peach orchard with one turn taking the cars perilously close to the cliff's edge near the river's shore. But its real claim to fame was that it was the highest and fastest coaster in the world.

The Blue Streak was designed for Woodcliff by engineer Vernon Keenan and was built by Joseph McKee. Keenan worked for Harry C. Baker Inc. of New York City and was a very sought-after designer and engineer of amusement rides, particularly roller coasters. He was commissioned to build the Blue Streak at about the same time he completed design work on the now historic Cyclone at Coney Island which also made its debut in 1927. The Cyclone and the Blue Streak shared some similarities. They were "out and back" coasters (end terminus met the starting point) constructed of wood, not unusual for the time. They were both chain-pulled up the first steep grade (many earlier "scenic railways" were manually pushed from a high point) where gravity then took over. The Blue Streak, however, boasted statistics that the Cyclone and its competitors would not surpass for decades.

Estimates of the Blue Streak's height ranged from 120 feet to 140 feet. Woodcliff Park's manager obviously preferred the latter figure. Its builder, Joseph McKee, conservatively estimated its height at 120 feet. *Popular Science Magazine* (1927) pegged it at 132 feet. Most likely, its height was between 120 and 130 feet above ground level. However, the highest drop into a ravine below grade added ten feet or so to the thrill ride. It sounds merely academic, but coaster enthusiasts were quick to hail the coaster as the highest in the world by far. Previous to the Blue Streak, the Racer at Chapultepec Park in Mexico City (110 feet high) was believed to be the highest. The Blue Streak's record remained intact until 1977 during the decade of the "coaster wars". Although long gone by that time, it relinquished its distinction to the "Beast" at Kings Island in Cincinnati, Ohio with a height of 141 feet. Estimates of the Blue Streak's length range from 2,000 feet to 3,200 feet.

The Blue Streak also held the coaster speed record for 54 years. With its top speed clocked at 65.2 miles per hour, the Blue Streak was finally surpassed in 1981 by the American Eagle coaster (66 miles per hour) at the Six Flags Great America Amusement Park in Gurnee, Illinois. No other coaster in history has held the height and speed records as long as the classic Blue Streak. Though some of today's steel coasters reach heights well over 300 feet and speeds up to 100 miles per hour, the Blue Streak remains a legend in amusement park history.

Another roller coaster called the Twister was constructed at a revamped Woodcliff in 1938. It was much lower to the ground and featured many hairpin turns. With its completion, the Woodcliff Pleasure Park's contributions to the "Golden Age of Coasters" were complete.

Ponty used a good potion of his capital (at least $90,000) to construct a huge swimming pool. The pool at Woodcliff was able to hold up to 3,000 bathers at a time. Ponty stated that the pool measured 50 by 200 foot although other accounts indicate a slightly smaller number. It's probable that Ponty expanded a pool that had been constructed by the Winslows around 1918. The pool opened in 1928 using Hudson River water. Its

Woodcliff Pleasure Park

modern filtration system led park managers to brag that the water was "...as pure and as crystal clear as the water you drink". Bathhouses were added in 1930 (they were destroyed by fire in 1948). It was generally regarded as one of the largest pools along the East Coast and probably one of the biggest in the country. For one dollar, a child could enjoy the rides, swim in the pool, and still have enough change left over to buy a hot dog. Despite those bargain prices, legend has it that adolescents regularly scaled the fences of the pool in order to save the separate ten cent admission cost. But the good times were short lived.

The Stock Market Crash of 1929 and the ensuing Great Depression years no doubt played heavily into the slow but steady decline of the Woodcliff Pleasure Park and many other amusement parks of the day. Disposable income for such frills as joy rides waned. In 1930 the dance hall burned and in 1932 the outdoor dance platform also burned, endangering the inn. Around this time renowned showman Jack Greenspan partnered with the Harry C. Baker Incorporated amusement firm and operated some concessions at Woodcliff.

Woodcliff tried to buck the economic trend and in 1934 it opened under new management headed by Brooklyn attorney Nicholas Dyruff. Title was eventually passed to Tempa E. Dyruff who bought the park at public auction on June 4, 1935 as Ponty's mortgage went into foreclosure. Nicholas Dyruff overhauled all of the rides, brought in a few new attractions, including a new roller skating rink, updated the swimming pool, and groomed the gardens and picnic areas. The refurbished Woodcliff Inn would now operate under separate management and it would expand to include an outdoor beer garden and dance area. The Twister coaster was added in 1938. Apparently it was not enough. The park struggled along into 1941.

While the Hudson River Day line excursions helped fill the park's coffers by bringing thousands of day trippers upriver from New York City each weekend, they had a great bearing on its abrupt and startling demise. A series of events occurred in 1941 from which the park never recovered.

In July 1941, a group of African Americans arrived from Manhattan and they were denied access to the swimming pool. The situation became racially charged. Rocks were hurled in and around the pool area. But that was just a prelude to the events of August 10, 1941.

The *State of Delaware* steamer arrived mid-afternoon carrying some 3,000 members of an Odd Fellows Lodge from New York City for their annual excursion up the Hudson River to Poughkeepsie. One thousand Polish Club members from nearby St. Joseph's Church were already occupying the inn (which they claimed they had reserved), the pool, and the part of the picnic area (which the New York City group claimed they had reserved). Several members of the city group were angered when they were refused beer at the inn. Other members entered the inn and began smashing windows and mirrors and upsetting furniture. The situation escalated as rocks and bottles were thrown into the pool injuring a child. Knives were drawn and even a hatchet was forcibly removed from a day tripper's grasp as locals fled the park. One police officer was stabbed. Reinforcements, including New York

Woodcliff Pleasure Park

State Police, were brought in to quell the riot but they were little match for the throngs. Before peace and quiet prevailed, four automobiles and several buildings were extensively damaged.

Key to restoring order was the blowing of the steamer's whistle. Most of the crowd which had arrived earlier on the *State of Delaware* ran to the boat thinking it was ready to depart. But several hundred persons stormed off the boat once again when they realized that several committee members were being detained for questioning. As more police reinforcements arrived, they were able to convince the visitors to reboard.

It is believed that the park never reopened after the riot of August 10, 1941. As a footnote, exactly one week later an even greater tragedy occurred. Another group from New York City had booked the *State of Delaware* originally with a scheduled stop at Woodcliff. But because of the previous week's trouble, the steamer planned merely to cruise upriver past West Point then return to New York City. Unbeknownst to the steamboat company, some 500 counterfeit tickets had materialized on the day of the excursion at the pier on West 131st Street. Since the boat was booked to capacity already, the ensuing chaos on the pier resulted in the trampling deaths of three women. Forty others were injured. To help alleviate the crush, New York City police allowed 1,250 or so of the 4,000 gathered to board. Most of those passengers never realized the unfortunate situation they left behind. Some were disconnected from loved ones until the steamer returned to port. Others reported that they had a "lovely" trip up and down the Hudson.

After the August 10th incidents, a hastened "safety" inspection of the park revealed dangers in the dock area and with the pedestrian bridge over the railroad tracks. Perhaps so, but the nearby communities were up in arms about security issues. The park ostensibly closed for repairs and a clean-up, but it never reopened. Fred Ponty was not around to witness the end of his beloved Woodcliff Pleasure Park. He died on June 19, 1941 just a few weeks before all the trouble began.

Shortly after its closure, the rides were dismantled. The now historic Blue Streak was taken down in 1942. The coaster's steel rails were donated to the war effort. Some of its planks were used by the Marist Brothers to build an apiary and a cannery in 1943. By 1944 the property still had a picnic grove, two gate houses, the main house, a barn, an outbuilding, and the pool.

The giant swimming pool arguably created the final battleground for the now unoccupied park. Serious consideration was given by the Town of Poughkeepsie to rehabilitate the pool and surrounding grounds to create a public park. Two factions evolved. One group was in favor of creating the park at Woodcliff. Alderman Detmer and his supporters felt the tab of $35,000 to purchase the property and some $25,000 to repair the pool, its pump, and the bathhouses would be preferable to building a new pool facility in downtown Poughkeepsie. Besides, he argued, picnic and parking areas were all in place. Supervisor Ross, on the other hand, felt that the repair costs were underestimated and argued in favor of the downtown location. He felt that the children of downtown Poughkeepsie deserved a facility close to their homes.

Woodcliff Pleasure Park

Civic groups, including scout groups, the Holy Name Society, and the Polish American Club became embroiled in the debate. Mayor Doran seemed to take the middle road by stating he liked the idea of purchasing Woodcliff but it needed to be self-supporting. The idea of a public subscription plan to defray costs was floated but it was eventually shelved. Ultimately, the pool at Woodcliff remained closed. Its remnants lingered and slowly deteriorated for decades, providing a haunting reminder of a once glorious period.

A February 1946 issue of *Billboard* noted that one Al Schlesinger of the Square Amusement Corporation and John Fitzgerald of JAFCO (a coin machine operation) from New York City had purchased the property, perhaps in a bid to rejuvenate the park, but there is no evidence that they ever acted on this alleged purchase. In 1948, the bathhouses were gutted by fire.

In the 1950s, the eastern portion of the Woodcliff parcel was purchased by Costanzo Construction. The firm housed its heavy equipment there and used the facilities for storage. They also leveled some of the terraces on the property. By this time, the mansion was gone although one of the Winslow estate's outbuildings with a grand billiards room was still intact.

Student residential housing was built on that same parcel starting around 1983. After that Marist College purchased the western half of the original property adjacent to the river to create athletic fields for its students.

Perhaps saddest of all, the quirky, ornate pink ticket house which enticed motorists traveling along Route 9 for many years was delicately dismantled, carefully labeled, and transported to Boscobel in Garrison where it was earmarked for reconstruction so it could be displayed on the grounds there. A storage house fire in the 1970s destroyed all the pieces before it was ever reassembled.

Woodcliff Pleasure Park

John Flack Winslow was born November 10, 1810 in Bennington, Vermont. He is best known for his contribution of money and expertise in the building of the Civil War ironclad warship the *Monitor*. When he retired in 1868 he purchased an estate in Poughkeepsie which later became Woodcliff Pleasure Park. *Drawing by Tatiana Rhinevault.*

The main house at the Winslow estate consisted of 35 rooms on three floors. Four staircases climbed to the watch tower which was 150 feet tall. The tower afforded a wonderful view of the river and the surrounding property. This house became the main restaurant of the park. Two girls stand outside the back of the house in this undated photograph. *Courtesy of Charles H. Wheeler.*

Lost Amusement Parks of the Hudson Valley

"WOOD-CLIFF"—RESIDENCE OF JOHN F. WINSLOW, ESQ., POUGHKEEPSIE, N. Y.

This poster shows two views of the Winslow mansion. The bottom picture shows the front of the house. The top picture shows the mansion on the left and the what might have been one of greenhouses on the right. *Courtesy of Charles H. Wheeler.*

Woodcliff Pleasure Park

After obtaining title to the former Winslow estate, entrepreneur Fred Ponty went about designing his dream amusement park. While some of the Winslow (and later Marian) buildings were demolished, others were kept and modified for the park's use. The Winslow mansion, seen on the left, was converted into the Woodcliff Inn which became an elegant venue for food, drink, music, and dance. Many of its interior features were preserved. It is sad to note that the inn was the focal point of a major disturbance that led to the park's closure in 1941. Little is known about the greenhouses on the right. *Author's collection.*

Construction workers pose by the nearly completed Blue Streak roller coaster in 1927. Master amusement designer Vernon Keenan was working on Coney Island's famous Cyclone coaster around the same time. They both began operation in 1927. While the Cyclone garnered most of the headlines, the Blue Streak became legendary in its own right. It went on to hold coaster height and speed records for decades. Joseph McKee was its builder.

It has often been reported that the park opened in 1918. However, there is much evidence to the contrary. As an example, this trophy was awarded at Woodcliff Pleasure Park in 1917. The trophy reads, "The Woodcliff Pleasure Park trophy won by Van's Dodgers Base Ball Club; Champions C.T.T.B League 1927". *Courtesy of Hunt Auctions.*

Woodcliff Pleasure Park

This wonderfully illustrated poster is the only one that can be found from the Woodcliff Pleasure Park era. Steamboats can be seen cruising the Hudson River at the top (looking west). Close scrutiny of the art work reveals such attractions as the Whip, the Caterpillar, the Scooter, the Frolic, the Ferris wheel, the Blue Streak roller coaster, a carousel, and a lovely domed dance pavilion. Along the bottom would be Albany Post Road (Route 9). Fred Ponty, president and general manager, was prone to bouts of hyperbole and superlatives just like many other amusement park proprietors of the time. But he was probably sincere when he declared that Woodcliff was the "most beautiful amusement resort" in the world. *Courtesy of James A. Cannavino Library, Archives and Special Collections, Marist College.*

Lost Amusement Parks of the Hudson Valley

The Blue Streak coaster dominates this overview of a portion of the park. To the right of the coaster is the swimming pool. The bath houses were completed in 1930. The grounds were beautifully landscaped and there were many areas for quiet strolls and picnics. The view is looking east. The one minute and ten second ride on the Blue Streak began with the chain lift followed by a rapid turnaround which led to a 70 foot drop then two smaller dips and some smaller hill drops. The track then led to a swooping fall towards a ravine which led to another fast turnaround perched on a cliff just above the Hudson River (it did not go out over the river as some reports claim). The climax of the ride followed. The cars returned to the coaster's full height then fell roughly 140 feet directly into the ravine, making the encroaching trees looked like blurs. Having just caught their breaths, one more drop would then lead the riders back to the station. *Author's collection.*

Woodcliff Pleasure Park

This postcard again reveals the beautifully groomed and thoughtfully designed grounds. Boat rentals were available for use on the lake. One of the several midways can be seen on the left. The building with the curved roof was a picnic area. *Courtesy of Larry Laliberte.*

Fred Ponty boasted that he had built the largest swimming pool in the eastern United States. However, the pool built at Indian Point (Buchanan) in 1929 just downriver may have been larger. The Woodcliff Pleasure Park's pool could accommodate roughly 3,000 bathers.

Lost Amusement Parks of the Hudson Valley

A crowded midway is shown in the postcard above. Most amusement parks during the early part of the twentieth century had a midway featuring penny arcades, shooting galleries, games of chance, photo galleries, food concessions, and the occasional side shows among other diversions. Woodcliff, a fairly large park for the era, was believed to have had three separate midways. Unlike amusement parks in heavily urban area, Woodcliff's ample acreage allowed for much open space as seen in the image below. Note the vendor at the bottom serving Hires root beer from the keg. Hires began production in 1876.

Woodcliff Pleasure Park

This advertisement was run to celebrate the opening of the Poughkeepsie-Highland Bridge (now the Mid-Hudson Bridge) in August 1930. There's little doubt that Ponty thought the new bridge would be a boon for business. There was ample parking across Albany Post Road to accommodate the influx of automobiles.

It is unknown what the Woodcliff Fun House Company, Inc. represented in this 1929 stock certificate. The president's name is somewhat illegible, but it definitely was not Fred Ponty. Ponty was still president and general manager of the park at that time. It is possible the company had a vested interest in a fun house within the park.

GRAND OPENING OF BALLROOM
At Woodcliff Pleasure Park
Season of 1929

On Saturday and Following Evening,
May 4 and 5
at 8 o'clock
Admission 50 Cents

Music by Al Hunter's Ten Piece Commodore Band

Come and have a wonderful evening's pleasure in an atmosphere of refinement and dance on the finest dance floor in the state

All Other Rides and Attractions in the Park Open These Days

WOODCLIFF PLEASURE PARK
Is Bigger, Better and Brighter than Ever

Fred Ponty also added a ballroom in Woodcliff's third year of operation. He claimed it was the largest in the state. His timing was good since the big brand era was just getting underway.

Woodcliff Pleasure Park

Hot dogs, wiener schnitzel, and bratwurst were featured at this lunch and refreshment stand. Again a Hires root beer keg can be observed on the left of the photograph. *Courtesy of Carney Rhinevault.*

Snappily dressed gentlemen pose in front of the Whip and the Blue Streak roller coaster. The Hudson River can be seen behind the tepee village and one of the midways. *Author's collection.*

Lost Amusement Parks of the Hudson Valley

The arched entrance and little pink ticket house were a fixture along Albany Post Road. Though the ticket house was earmarked for preservation, its dismantled and labeled pieces were destroyed by fire in the 1970s. *Courtesy of Carney Rhinevault.*

The fire of June 13, 1932 was controlled quickly enough so that damage to the inn was minimal. However the outdoor dance platform was destroyed. It was quickly rebuilt.

Woodcliff Pleasure Park

The Woodcliff Pleasure Park hosted numerous athletic events including boxing, wrestling, baseball, and equestrian contests. Boxing matches were particularly well-attended. Light-heavyweight Melio Bettina was a local favorite. He was a long-time resident of Beacon who, for a time, held the light-heavy-weight championship of the world (1939) as recognized by the New York State Athletic Commission. Between 1938 and 1939, Bettina fought at Woodcliff three times. He won all three. The unorthodox left-handed style of Bettina baffled opponents. He retired in 1948 and earned a spot in the World Boxing Hall of Fame in 1995. He passed away a year after this honor. Here he poses with the great Joe Louis at Camp Shanks in Rockland County during World War II. *Courtesy of the Orangetown Historic Museum and Archives. Photograph by U.S. Army Signal Corps.*

Lost Amusement Parks of the Hudson Valley

This recent aerial view shows the area that was once the Woodcliff Pleasure Park. Marist College's student housing, parking lots, and athletic field now dominate the landscape. This view is looking north. The Hudson River is off to the left of the athletic field. The overlays show where the little pink ticket house was located (top right, along Route 9), the Blue Streak roller coaster (upper left), the swimming pool just below the coaster, and the two bridges and a tunnel (along the left side) which were access points for visitors who arrived on steamships. *Photograph from the collection of Carney Rhinevault. Overlays by Carney Rhinevault.*

Orange Lake Park

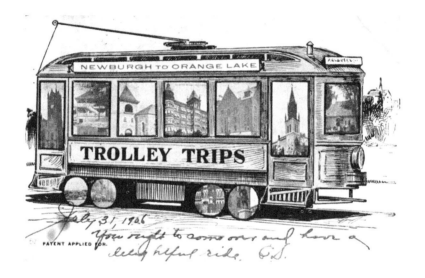

The amusement park at Orange Lake was located in Orange County about six miles west of Newburgh, New York. It had always been a place where people could enjoy fishing, boating, swimming and a pleasant walk   People traveled to the lake either on horseback or in horse-driven carriages. The advent of trolley service greatly increased the park's popularity and led to it becoming one of the most popular parks in the northeast.

The Haines brothers, David S., John D., Charles D., Elmer T., and Andrew G. came to Newburgh on November 23, 1886 to build a street railway. They named their company the Newburgh Street Railroad Company. They were successfully able to lay trolley tracks in Newburgh in a span of one month despite the fact that there was a two foot frost. Their first trolley line began running on December 23, 1886. In those early days the trolleys were on tracks drawn by horses. The original line ran from the western end of the city to the riverfront.

Over the years trolley service expanded in the city of Newburgh with lines running north and south instead of merely east-west. After electricity effectively replaced horse power, in June 1894 the system was renamed the Newburgh Electric Railway. This change from horse power to electric power caused a tremendous expansion of service. People no longer had to jump off overloaded cars so that the horses could pull the heavy cars up Broadway, a steep hill in Newburgh. The concomitant reduction of noise made the trips on the trolleys a much more enjoyable experience as well

On May 29, 1895, an expanded trolley line made its first trip from Newburgh to Walden. On board were the president of the line, Benjamin Norton, and other dignitaries including Benjamin Barker Odell Jr., then-former Governor of New York. On their return to Newburgh from Walden the passengers were treated to dinner at the Palatine Hotel where landlord H. N. Bain prepared the finest of banquets. The Orange Lake Traction Company owned and operated these lines. Trolleys ran from 6 AM to 11 PM making many trips to Walden every day. They stopped along the way at Glenwood Park and Orange Lake. At Glenwood Park there was a small hotel, a pavilion, and a merry-go-round. There were 15 open cars for warm weather and two enclosed cars for winter use. The trip from Newburgh to Orange Lake cost ten cents in 1895.

Orange Lake Park

The trolley was also used to carry freight from Walden to the Newburgh waterfront. Often the freight was then shipped to New York City. In 1896, 50,000 cans of milk were transported in closed cars. In the summer these cars were chilled with ice to keep the milk fresh. The trolley company charged between five and seven and a half cents a can to carry the milk. Condensed milk from the Borden Company was carried on trolley cars as well. The trolley also carried countless apples and potatoes, 1,000 tons of hay and between 100 and 200 tons of grapes in 1896. In addition the United States mail was carried on trolleys three or four times a day. Freight and mail service made up 38 percent of the gross receipts for the company in 1896.

Orange Lake Park occupied 38 acres at the southern end of the 400 acre lake. People would travel to the park from New York City, Albany, Kingston, Poughkeepsie, and other river towns. Odell was on the board of the Orange Lake Traction Company (and at times its president) and president of the Central Hudson Steamship Company. The Central Hudson Steamship Company had a fleet of ten steamboats which operated between Albany and New York City. Visitors would often take a steamboat to Newburgh where they would board trolleys for the 15-to 20 minute ride to the lake. Odell's steamboat passengers, as well as passengers on the Hudson River Dayline, could purchase a round trip ticket on a steamboat boat plus a free pass on the trolley for a dollar.

When Odell took over the Orange Lake Traction Company in 1906, he continued developing Orange Lake Park into a showcase. Not only were there many amusements for visitors to enjoy but the vistas around the lake were quite lovely. Each year he added new forms of entertainment, including a roller-skating rink, snack bars, a midway with games of chance, a Ferris wheel, a public beach for swimming, and row boats and canoes for rent. Near the shore was a children's playground with traditional swings. Visitors could come for the day or stay for an extended visit in one of the bungalows dotting the lakeside.

The park opened every year on Decoration Day (presently called Memorial Day) and closed around Labor Day. A theatre located at the lake provided both musical and comedy acts. On opening day, May 30, 1911, the park advertised J.M. Moore's New Orleans Minstrels. The program included four big vaudeville acts and the Globe Comedy Four. This was one of the many African-American troupes that entertained in a variety of venues around the country.

Every afternoon and evening there was dancing in the open air dance pavilion on the lake's shore. People would often come to dance and have dinner in the park. For 75 cents one could enjoy a table d'hote or a fixed price multi-coursed dinner in the park's restaurant.

Famous music artists including Ozzie Nelson, Tommy Dorsey, Benny Goodman, and Ward Harrison performed at the park's bandstand. Odell prohibited the sale of alcohol at the park. He wanted the park to be a family-friendly place where only people of refinement came. The park had picnic groves which could be rented by large groups for community and local events. There was also a rambling path through the trees that locals referred to as Flirtation Walk or Lovers Lane.

Orange Lake Park

One of the rides was the Ye Olde Mill. In this ride passengers rode in boats which floated on tracks and took them through dark tunnels. People who remember the park said that this was a scary ride. Other rides such as the Jack Rabbit were much tamer. This ride was a small scenic railway with a few small hills.

After Benjamin's death on May 9, 1926, his estate sold the property to the Orange Lake Development Corporation for $45,000. Many of the park's concessionaires had leases which were not set to expire until May 1, 1934. The park continued operating under amusement park impresario Edward E. Rhoads, who controlled Edward Rhoads' Amusement Park in Wildwood, New Jersey and Carsonia Park in Reading, Pennsylvania. Unfortunately for Rhoads, he bought these parks just before the stock market crashed in 1929. Rhoads' failing health forced him to retire in 1932. He leased the park to Howard T. Levan who opened the park for the Memorial Day weekend in 1933.

Levan added free bathing, an auto ride, the Linda Loop, the Troupe of Monkeys, and the Hey Day ride. In 1937 Levan purchased the park from Rhoads for $50,000. However, even with the new attractions, financial difficulties could not be overcome.

Like most trolley parks of the era, Orange Lake Park saw a chain reaction of factors which led to its demise. As the use of automobiles increased it allowed people the freedom to travel further from home to more varied places. As a result the effects were felt in both steamboat and trolley travel along the Hudson. Compounded with the construction of the George Washington Bridge, the

Bear Mountain Bridge and the Newburgh Beacon Bridge connecting the east and west shores of the Hudson River made it no longer profitable for boat companies to continue their runs up and down the river.

During the Great Depression, the park was forced to close for a number of years. The park was eventually dismantled in 1941 when the realty company of Copans and Levinson announced plans to build homes at the lake. The plan provided for 30 lakefront lots and 60 more lots set back from the beach. The lots set back would have access to a 100 foot beach on the lake. Today Orange Lake is a residential community with homes along the lake. Nothing remains of the amusement park that brought tens of thousands of visitors to enjoy the lake and the area around it.

Orange Lake Park

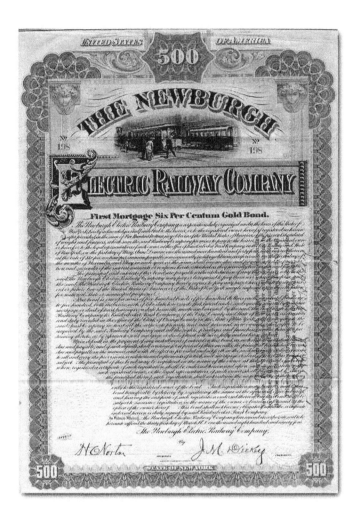

The original trolleys in Newburgh were horse-drawn. In 1894 when the trolleys went from horse power to electric power, the company changed its name to the Newburgh Electric Railway Company. The company offered bonds to give it operating capital. This bond certificate is a $500 mortgage bond. A mortgage bond is secured by real property. It was part of a $250,000 bond issue dated May1, 1894 running until May 1, 1944. The bond was payable every May and November at the offices of the Knickerbocker Trust Company of New York, who was the trustee of the mortgage.

Lost Amusement Parks of the Hudson Valley

Benjamin Barker Odell Jr. was born 1854 in Newburgh, New York. He died in May 1926. Odell was the Governor of New York from 1901 to 1904. He was also president of the Central Hudson Steamship Company. When he became president of the Orange Traction Company in 1906 he developed Orange Lake Park into a major destination for fun seekers.

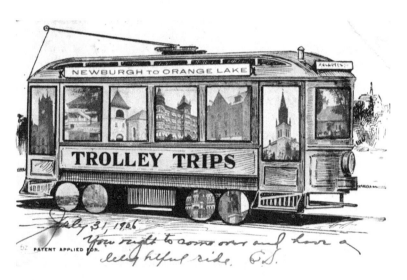

In 1895, trolley service was expanded from Newburgh to Walden. Trolleys stopped at Orange Lake, which was half way between the two cities. The postcard shown here was sent July 31, 1906 and depicts a trolley car. Scenes of Newburgh can be seen on the windows and wheels of the car. *Courtesy of Carla Decker.*

Orange Lake Park

People are arriving at Orange Lake Park by trolley. The postcard above shows one of the closed trolley cars that ran on the Newburgh to Orange Lake line. The one below shows open trolley cars which ran in the warm weather. *Courtesy of Carla Decker.*

Lost Amusement Parks of the Hudson Valley

ENTRANCE TO ORANGE LAKE PARK, NEWBURGH, N. Y.

The building in this postcard is the waiting room at the Orange Lake Park trolley station. Notice the open trolley gate to allow the passengers to enter the park. *Courtesy of Carla Decker.*

This view of the waiting room is from inside the park. It reveals both an indoor and outdoor area for people to wait for a return trolley to Newburgh. *Courtesy of Carla Decker.*

Orange Lake Park

The waiting room is on the right and the roller skating rink is on the left in this postcard. Rolling skating was offered every afternoon and evening at the lake. *Courtesy of Carla Decker.*

When arriving at the lake people were greeted by many booths selling postcards, souvenirs, ice cream, candy, peanuts, cold non-alcoholic beverages, and other refreshments. *Courtesy of Carla Decker.*

Lost Amusement Parks of the Hudson Valley

One of the most popular activities at Orange Lake were the band concerts. Ozzie Nelson, Tommy Dorsey, Benny Goodman, and Ward Harrison in addition to many other bands performed at the lake. An Orange Lake Park advertisement in the *Newburgh Evening Union* on June 14, 1911 mentions free band concerts every Sunday at 3 PM, weather permitting. On special occasions, such as the 4th Fourth of July, concerts were also held at night, as the card below shows. *Above courtesy of Gary Ferguson; below courtesy of Carla Decker.*

Orange Lake Park

VISITORS WAITING FOR ROW BOATS, ORANGE LAKE PARK, NEWBURGH, N. Y.

A major attraction at the lake was boating and fishing. In addition to the main boat house, several entrepreneurs offered row boats and canoes for rent. The above postcard shows visitors waiting to get aboard one of the many row boats for rent. Below people are enjoying a gentle paddle on the lake in their canoes. *Above courtesy of Gary Ferguson; below courtesy of Carla Decker.*

Lost Amusement Parks of the Hudson Valley

The boat house is shown in the postcard above. The upper floor had a restaurant and an area for dancing. On the lower floor was a storage area for the boats. On the far left you can see the shoot-the-chutes. The bottom card is a close up of the shoot-the-chutes, spelled shoot-the-shoots on the card. Orange Lake's version of this ride was a giant water slide. At other parks, small boats would take visitors down the chute like a present day flume ride. *Courtesy of Gary Ferguson.*

Orange Lake Park

The Park Restaurant advertised that you could get a full course dinner there for 75 cents. The sign on the restaurant stated "votes for women". In the foreground is a souvenir shop that advertised that you could check your parcels. *Courtesy of Gary Ferguson.*

In addition to the park restaurant there was a Japanese Tea garden. Tea gardens served tea and light fare in a peaceful garden-like setting. This postcard shows the tea garden on the left and roller skating rink on the right. *Courtesy of Carla Decker*

SIGHT SEEING LAUNCH. ORANGE LAKE. NEWBURGH. N. Y.

The naphtha-powered sightseeing boat passes by the boat house in this postcard. It took passengers on a half-hour spin on the lake. The boat was also used to bring people to and from the cottages and hotels around the lake. The canopy provided shade on warm summer days. *Courtesy of Carla Decker.*

Near the boat house was a children's playground with conventional swings. On the right hand side of the picture is the carousel. *Courtesy of Carla Decker*

Orange Lake Park

THE "MIDWAY," ORANGE LAKE PARK, NEWBURGH, N. Y.

The top postcard shows the midway at Orange Lake Park. The midway had rides, games of chance, and refreshment stands. At the left edge of the card and below you can see the Jack Rabbit ride. This was a gentle rolling train ride around the grounds. Notice that the cards were taken at two different times, as the rabbit icon appears different in each of them. *Courtesy of Gary Ferguson.*

ENJOYING THE "JACK RABBIT," ORANGE LAKE PARK, NEWBURGH, N. Y.

ENJOYING THE MUSIC AT THE BAND STAND, ORANGE LAKE PARK, NEWBURGH, N. Y.

The Ferris wheel which can be seen in these postcards is probably the same one taken from different angles. The top one shows the band stand in the foreground with people milling around enjoying the music. In the bottom card on the left hand side a souvenir stand selling postcards can be seen. *Above courtesy of Gary Ferguson; below courtesy of Carla Decker.*

VISITING EXCURSIONISTS ARRIVING AT THE PARK, ORANGE LAKE PARK, NEWBURGH, N. Y.

Orange Lake Park

This ride is called the swinger, airplane ride, circle swing, or swing carousel. This is a popular family amusement ride which has survived the test of time. It is often seen in traveling carnivals as well as regular amusement parks. *Courtesy of Carla Decker.*

Lost Amusement Parks of the Hudson Valley

Note on this postcard the name of the swinger ride is the "airplane ride". The swings on it have been replaced with airplanes. Next to the airplane ride is a Ferris wheel. *Courtesy of Carla Decker.*

Another ride at Orange Lake Park was the Ye Olde Mill. This was a boat ride through a series of dark tunnels. Sometimes this ride is referred to as the "tunnel of love." *Courtesy of Carla Decker.*

Orange Lake Park

FERRIS WHEEL, ORANGE LAKE PARK, NEWBURGH, N. Y.

The postcards on these two pages show two different Ferris wheels at Orange Lake Park. In this Ferris wheel four people, all facing forward, can ride in a single car. *Courtesy of Gary Ferguson.*

Each car in this Ferris wheel seats two people. *Courtesy of Carla Decker.*

Orange Lake Park

Not only did the park have amusements but it also had a bathing beach near the boat house. The second floor of the boat house had lockers for the the use of swimmers. A group of children appear to be enjoying the water while a couple paddles by in their canoe. *Courtesy of Gary Ferguson.*

The penny arcade at Orange Lake Park was a popular attraction judging from this undated postcard. Penny arcades traditionally included small movies which were a series of cards that flipped in quick succession. They also had early pinball or other simple mechanical devices which required a penny to operate. *Courtesy of Carla Decker.*

Lost Amusement Parks of the Hudson Valley

The interior of the dance pavilion is shown in this postcard. Advertisements in the *Newburgh Evening Union* in June 1911 announced that dancing was offered at the lake every Wednesday and Saturday evening at 8 PM. *Courtesy of Carla Decker.*

The theatre at the lake provided entertainment every night at 8 PM and matinees on Wednesdays and Saturdays at 3 PM. The entertainment included some of the most notable actors and actresses of the time. *Courtesy of Carla Decker.*

Orange Lake Park

Orange Lake Park advertised its events in the *Newburgh Evening Union*. This advertisement from the June 10, 1911 paper represents a typical one. In this advertisement Dan Crimmins and Rosa Gore perform in the musical comedy "A Warm Match." This comedy, was to quote the *New York Times,* "a hodgepodge of nonsense, which fun is provided by the clowning of the man and the remarkable personality of the woman." *Courtesy of the Newburgh Evening Union.*

Lost Amusement Parks of the Hudson Valley

Orange Lake provided ample space for visitors to enjoy a picnic while taking in the bucolic surroundings. If you chose not to bring along a lunch many food concession stands filled the bill. Below a couple enjoys a bit of privacy in another area of the park. *Courtesy of Carla Decker.*

Orange Lake Park

TWELFTH ANNUAL

COMMUNITY OUTING

Orange Lake Park

WEDNESDAY, AUGUST 7, 1929

*Conducted for the People of Newburgh
by the Newburgh Chamber of Commerce*

— THE PROGRAM —

AFTERNOON—ONE O'CLOCK

CONCERT—Ortone's Band
BABY BEAUTY SHOW
PARADE DECORATED DOLL AND BABY CARRIAGES
TRUE ROMANCE CONTEST
DOG SHOW
OUTBOARD MOTOR BOAT RACING
CANOE TILTING
CANOE RACING
ROWBOAT RACING
SPEED ROLLER SKATING EXHIBITION
  Tom Longfield, formerly world's professional champion
SKIDWAY JUMPING
BALLOON ASCENSION AND PARACHUTE JUMPING

EVENING—SIX O'CLOCK

CONCERT—D'AGOSTINO'S BAND
BALLOON ASCENSION AND ILLUMINATED PARACHUTE JUMP
ILLUMINATED BOAT PARADE
FIREWORKS
COMMUNITY CARNIVAL DANCE—Rose Garden Pavilion

EXHIBITORS

"Goods Made and Sold in Newburgh"

John Schoonmaker & Son, Inc., The Newburgh News, Hewitt & Warden, Atwater-Kent Radio and Washing Machines; Fred Michaels, Decorative Iron Urns; Smith & Clark, Ice Cream; Orange County Bottling Works, Premium Pride Fruit Beverages; Fletcher Bros., Kelvinator Refrigeration; Hi-Land Bread Co., Bread and Cake; Highlands Electric Co., General Electric Refrigeration; Newburgh Auto Sales Co., Ford-Lincoln Cars; Shapiro Sporting Goods Co., Outboard Motor Boats; Stanley Brundage, Colonial Radios.

GENERAL COMMITTEE

Harry Cohen, Chairman; John E. Drew, Treasurer; Orin C. Baker, Secretary; John F. Tucker, Arthur E. Brundage, F. A. Munger, Fred Stern, Arthur M. Palmer, Walter S. Carvey, Lawrence Taft, Harry D. Calyer, Douglas P. Miller, Walter Haible, E. C. Maloney, Dr. A. J. Allot, William T. McCaw, B. Bryant Odell, Augustus Bennet, President, Newburgh Chamber of Commerce.

Many events were held at the park, hosted by local community groups and groups from further away. This is the cover of a program for an outing "For the People of Newburgh.". The event was sponsored by the Chamber of Commerce in Newburgh. There were afternoon and evening events planned as well as exhibits by merchants from Newburgh. The event day culminated with a boat parade, fireworks, and a dance. *Courtesy of the Newburgh Free Library.*

Orange Lake Park

Visitors could come to Orange Lake for a day or stay longer in one the many bungalows or hotels that surrounded the lake. These two postcards show "The Cove" or "Millers Cove". People staying at the lake could enjoy the many activities at the park. *Courtesy of Carla Decker.*

Indian Point Park

The era of steamboats led to the creation of Indian Point Park in Buchanan, New York. The park was a product of the Hudson River Day Line company, one of the largest steamboat companies on the Hudson River from 1863 until 1948. It was created by the steamboat company to generate more revenue for its coffers.

Since Robert Fulton first sailed from New York City to Albany in 1807, steamboats became fixtures on the Hudson River until fairly recent times. They carried passengers not only between New York and Albany but also between other ports along the river. During this time period, large communities developed along the river bringing with them the necessity of river transportation. Many of these communities like Troy, Poughkeepsie and Newburgh supported steamboat lines which traveled between them and New York City. It was into this mix that Abraham Van Santvoord arrived. Van Santvoord wanted to be the main provider of steamboat service between Albany and New York. In 1863, Van Santvoord, John McBride Davidson, and Chauncey Vibbard formed a partnership and purchased the steamboats *Daniel Drew* and *Armenia.* The next year they added a brand new steamer called the *Chauncey Vibbard*.

In 1879, Van Santvoord and Davidson incorporated their holdings and named the company the Hudson River Line. The company continued to concentrate on its New York-to-Albany run by adding several new steamboats to their fleet. These included the *New York* built in 1887 and the *Albany* built in 1880. The name of the company became the Hudson River Day Line by order of the Supreme Court of New York in August 1899.

Eben Erskine Olcott, Van Santvoord's son-in-law, became president of the Hudson River Day Line in 1902. Under his leadership the company added the *Hendrick Hudson* in 1906, the *Robert Fulton* in 1909, and the largest day liner of all, the *Washington Irving,* in 1913.

The Hudson River Day Line had always believed that the more they offered their passengers, the more passengers would avail themselves of the boats. In 1923 the company decided that they needed to create a new destination for their passengers. Many passengers sailed to Bear Mountain for the day aboard the Day Line.

However once they left the ship, the Day Line would lose all revenue until the return trip. But if the company owned the park it could continue making money all day rather than from the voyage alone.

The company selected a piece of land, the site of a defunct brickyard, for its park. It was located about 40 miles north of New York City on the eastern shore of the Hudson River, in the Town of Buchanan just south of Peekskill. The property consisted of 320 acres of riverfront land. No doubt the park was designed after the popular "pleasure gardens" in Europe.

The company named the park Indian Point Park because they learned that the Kitchawank tribe once walked there. Once developed, the privately-owned park contained wooded paths for strolling, picnic tables, and places to enjoy a quiet walk along the river. A cafeteria provided food and drinks for the visitors. The facilities included a beach along the river with a specially-marked area. A playground was built for children near the river. Children could enjoy a refreshing swing, a ride on a seesaw, a slide, or a turn on the hand-pushed merry-go-rounds. Part of the property was used as a farm where fresh vegetables were grown for the kitchens of the Day Line's boats and the restaurants in the park.

The bell from the *Mary Powell* was placed along the shore and was rung to announce the arrival and departures of the steamers. The *Mary Powell* was a steamboat that had been built in 1861. She was owned by Van Santvoord and Davidson, the founders of the Hudson River Day Line, and operated from 1861 to 1919 when she was finally scrapped.

Indian Point Park

The owners of the Day Line wanted their park to be a pleasant and welcome place for visitors. They wanted to provide a haven where people could enjoy fresh air and escape from the hustle and bustle of city life. Indian Point Park became such a place. Not only were the surroundings beautiful but the park was a peaceful and relaxing place to spend the day. It was even designed to be accessible for the handicapped so that even the wheelchair-bound could enjoy a day at the park.

In 1929, a swimming pool measuring 100 by 150 feet was built. The pool was one of largest around. It had its own bathhouse and lockers for 1,500 guests. Admission to the pool was ten cents if you entered before 11:00 AM, 25 cents after.

Local boys remember going to Indian Point Park in time to meet the boats arriving from New York. The more adventurous ones waited in the water as the boats were docking and encouraged the girls to throw pennies into the water. The boys would dive to retrieve them and later they would try to find the girl at the swimming pool and return the pennies to her. If they were lucky they would get to spend the day in her company until it was time for her boat to sail home.

After World War II, automobiles became more affordable. People no longer needed to travel by river boat or rail to escape to the country. They could travel freely in their own private vehicles. The Hudson River Day Line found itself losing revenue. The company raised the fare from New York to Albany from two dollars to three dollars one-way and from four dollars to five dollars for a round trip. This helped alleviate the financial drain to a degree but the company realized it was time to sell the business. In 1948, the company announced it was going out of business.

The company's property in Buchanan including Indian Point Park was auctioned off in October 1949. H. M. Margolis of Shore Hill Estates purchased two parcels totaling 232 acres for $106,000 and K.B. Weissman of New Rochelle purchased a third parcel totaling 52 acres for $11,000. Margolis' parcel included the amusement park. He later sold the parcel to Emanuel D. Kelmans who reopened the park on May 20, 1950.

When Kelmans began operating the park it contained three rides and two concessions. Each year he doubled or tripled the amusements and concessions in the park. By 1952, the park had 50 concessions. The park now included five ball fields, a beer hall, restaurant facilities, concession stands, a dance hall, amusement rides, an outdoor arena, a new midway, speed boats, row boats, a picnic area with fireplaces, a roller skating rink, miniature golf, and a driving range. Some of the rides included the scooter cars, a merry-go-round, the Double Looper, the Caterpillar, a chair plane, the Jumping Jack, Little Dipper, fire engine, hot rods, and a whip. The park also had kiddie rides, including a merry-go-round, jeeps, a fire engine, a Ferris wheel, boats and a miniature train. Admission to the park was 25 cents and ten cents extra for a speed boat ride.

During the first year the park drew daily crowds of up to 15,000. The park could accommodate 1,000 cars. People traveled from up and down the Hudson Valley and from New York City. A local bus ran to the park from the town of Peekskill. Kelmans drew in New York City residents by placing advertisements in city newspapers. Kelmans even placed a billboard on Broadway in Manhattan. He also planned to have amateur night every Friday evening for the duration of the season. The winner would win a two-week performance engagement at Indian Point Park.

Starting in 1950, Kelmans also had a tie-in with Coca-Cola. Whenever Coca-Cola advertised locally on the radio, the spot included a mention of Indian Point Park. In exchange, only Coca-Cola products were sold at the park. At this time two boats came to the park each day in addition to charter tours.

Many local people employed at the park felt their stint at Indian Point Park was more fun than work, and more than a few workers reportedly met their spouses at Indian Point Park. In 1952 and 1953, the Westchester County Fair was held at Indian Point Park. It had been one of Kelmans' ideas to revive this tradition. The fair was under the sponsorship of the Westchester Horticultural and Agricultural Association. In 1952, Kelmans started keeping the park opened on weekend nights. This was done to allow more Westchester residents access to the park after the steamships had departed for the day. On nights when the park was open, guests were treated to fireworks, barn dances, and roller-skating. All the other amusement facilities remained open as well. He also placed advertisements in local newspapers with coupons that allowed local residents admission to the park, roller rink, and swimming pool for 35 cents Monday through Friday.

The estimated attendance in 1951 was 300,000 people. By 1952, the expectation was that 400,000 people would come to the park based on advanced reservations from various groups. School and college groups traveled from as far away as Philadelphia. Indian Point, which had once relied on day boat transportation, was seeing car and bus visitors outnumber boaters by two to one. As many as 90 buses at a time parked at Indian Point.

After owning Indian Point Park for five years, Kelmans sought to sell the property. Consolidated Edison Gas and Electric Company was looking for property near New York City. It was planning to build a new power plant to provide for the growing electrical needs of New York City. In October 1954, Consolidated Edison bought the property for $250,000. At the time of the sale, Kelmans promised that the park would remain open for at least two more years to give his concessionaires a chance to relocate. Kelmans had taken a park the Hudson River Day Line operated mainly as a pleasure park and had turned it into a full scale amusement park.

Before the park's closure, The Cristiani brothers planned to bring their circus to Creek Hill Park in the nearby Town of Cortlandt in 1956. Due to a large advance ticket sale, they realized they would need to use their biggest tent. Unfortunately, the giant tent was too large for the intended space at Creek Hill Park. The Cristiani Brothers Circus was moved to Indian Point Park, and the attendance at the evening show was between 3,000 and 5,000 people. More than 150 boys and girls from the St. Joseph's Home in Peekskill, an orphanage run by the Franciscan Nuns, attended. The circus would be the last large event ever held at Indian Point Park.

Indian Point Park

The landscape would soon morph dramatically. In the fall of 1962, the first nuclear reactor began to generate electricity. This reactor became known as Indian Point I. It was the first privately-financed commercial nuclear reactor in the United States. Since that time, two reactors, Indian Point II and Indian Point III, have been added to the site. In 1975, Consolidated Edison sold Indian Point III to the New York Power Authority. In 2000, the New York Power Authority in turn sold its reactor to Entergy in 2001, Consolidated Edison followed suit. Entergy now owns and operates all three nuclear reactors on the former site of Indian Point Park.

Today all that remains of the park is part of a stairway that once led to the swimming pool and an empty lot that was once a ball field.

Lost Amusement Parks of the Hudson Valley

The Hudson River Dayline Company built Indian Point Park to enhance their revenue. The park began as a pleasure park with lovely relaxing scenery and a beach for swimming. This postcard shows the boat landing and picnic area at the park. *Courtesy of Gail and Mike Ruh.*

Looking from the west the pier is shown on the left. On the right side of the photograph along the shore is the dance pavilion. The other buildings on the hillside were snack bars, the restaurant and the first aid station. *Courtesy of Brian Vangor.*

Indian Point Park

These two postcards show some of the parks many walkways. On the right of the top card a children's playground with swings and two hand pushed merry-go-rounds can be seen. On the card below the top of the dance pavilion can be seen through the trees. On the right side is a day liner at the dock. *Above courtesy of Gail and Mike Ruh, below courtesy of Town of Buchanan William J. Burke Historical Room.*

The terrace at Indian Point was a gently rolling hill where visitors can relax and enjoy the river breezes. *Courtesy of Brian Vangor.*

This aerial view shows the docks on the left side (notice the day liner pulling away from the dock) and athletic fields (circled on the card). The building with the roof is the swimming pool built in 1929. *Courtesy of Gail and Mike Ruh.*

Indian Point Park

The Washington Irving the largest day liner of them all made frequent stops at Indian Point. It was a steel hulled ship built by the New York Shipbuilding Corporation in Camden New Jersey. The ship was 414 feet long and 86 feet wide over all and could handle 6,600 passengers. When it was launched on December 17, 1912 the Mascot Club from Washington Irving High School was invited to attend. Years before the club was started by a redhead from the school who had heard that good luck follows the head of the redheaded maiden. It seems that the school had been promised a new building but nothing ever came of it. A redheaded student organized all the redheads and near-redheads into the Mascot Club. The club attended a Board of Estimate meeting and sat there with their fingers crossed throughout the meeting. Their lucky charm worked. The school got a new building. From that time on, the club was a fixture at the school. *Author's collection.*

Lost Amusement Parks of the Hudson Valley

Approximately 50 members of the club attended the launching of the *Washington Irving* as guests of the Day Line. They traveled on a private train from New York dubbed the "Redheaded Special." The railroad found a redheaded engineer to drive the train for the occasion. The girls were chaperoned by their principal, William McAndrew, who happened to be a redhead as well. The redheads all wore white sweaters and a red sash with "WIHS" on it. On their heads were wreaths of ivy from Washington's Irving home in Sunnydale. The ivy was from a plant supposedly given to Washington Irving by Sir Walter Scott. Mrs. Eben E. Olcott christened the ship with a bottle of water which came from Washington Irving's well. When she raised the bottle the girls all stood on tip-toe and raised their crossed fingers over their heads. The club was such a hit that they were invited to attend an invitation-only cruise on the Hudson River on May 14, 1913. They once again dressed in white with blue ribbons tied in their hair. Two days later the entire student body of Washington Irving High was invited to sail up the river to Washington Irving's home at Sunnydale consuming 75 gallons of lemonade along the way. *Courtesy of Robert Ferguson.*

Indian Point Park

The Washington Irving settles to the bottom at Jersey City

The *Washington Irving* met an unexpected and tragic ending on June 1, 1926. Captain David H. Deming was piloting as the ship left DesBrosses Street in New York. He gave a long blast of her whistle signaling to other ships she was getting underway. There was heavy traffic in the harbor that morning including a U.S. army lighter carrying troops and the tugboat *Thomas E. Moran* towing two oil barges. Captain Deming signaled one blast to indicate that he planned to cut across the bow of both boats. The lighter went around the stern of the *Washington Irving*. The tug and barges did not turn until the last minute. The *Washington Irving* struck the side of one of the barges and tore a 20 foot hole in her side. Two of the six watertight bulkheads were ripped open and water rushed into the ship. The Captain sounded a distress signal and was able to bring the ship across the river to the Erie Railroad's Pier 9 in New Jersey. The ship sank and it was discovered that three of the people on board were missing. Mrs. Hoag, her three year old daughter Mary and a former mess boy were not found. The Hudson River Day Line determined the damage to the Washington Irving made her unsalvageable and left the ship where she sank. The ship remained there until 1933 when she was finally sold for scrap. *Courtesy of Robert Ferguson.*

Lost Amusement Parks of the Hudson Valley

The *Washington Irving* not only was the largest of the day liners but it was also the fanciest one too. It had a deck which was based on Spain's Alhambra with individual cubicles and wooden writing decks. One of the decks had an art gallery with paintings of the Hudson River Valley. This photograph shows the upper deck of the *Washington Irving* as it heads up the Hudson River. *Author's collection.*

The bell from the *Mary Powell* was placed near the shore it rang to announce the arrival of the day liners. This served as a welcome to the ships and alerted workers to the arrival of new visitors to the park. The Reserve Fleet or moth ball fleet which was at Jones Point from 1946 until 1970 can be seen across the river. *Courtesy of Town of Buchanan William J. Burke Historical Room.*

Indian Point Park

A pool was added to the park in 1929. The pool measured 100 X 150 feet making it one of the largest pools along the east coast. The postcard above shows three gentlemen relaxing outside the pool. Below the pool is shown on a crowded day. *Above courtesy of Brian Vangor; below courtesy of Town of Buchanan William J. Burke Historical Room.*

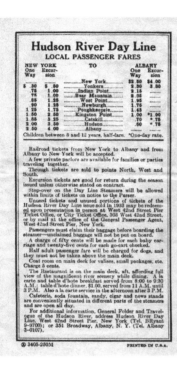

Indian Point Park

In October 1949 the firm of Joseph P. Day Inc. was hired by the Hudson River Day Line to sell their Indian Point Park property. Joseph's company was well known in the real estate auction market. In 1904 it was estimated that over half the land sold in New York was sold at auction. During his career, Day's company sold about one third of the land in the Bronx and one third of the land in Queens. In the center of this photograph auctioneer McDonald of Day's company is shown. *Courtesy of Town of Buchanan William J. Burke Historical Room.*

After the auction the parcel containing the park was resold to Emanuel D. Kelmans. Kelmans reopened the park on May 1, 1950. The ribbon cutting for the new park is shown in this photograph. Pictured (left to right) are an unknown Buchanan Trustee, Mayor William J. Burke, Jules Logelin, Emanuel J. Kelmans, George Foster, and Walter Hoffman. *Courtesy of Town of Buchanan William J. Burke Historical Room.*

Indian Point Park

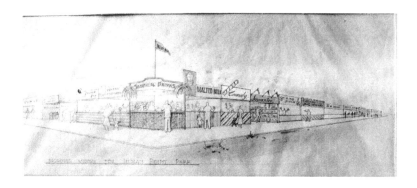

When Kelmans bought the park in 1949 he redesigned it from a pleasure park to a real amusement park. The drawing above shows the proposed plan for a new midway at Indian Point. The photograph below shows the finished midway when the park reopened in 1950. *Courtesy of Town of Buchanan William J. Burke Historical Room.*

Lost Amusement Parks of the Hudson Valley

A Hudson River Day Liner pulls into the dock at Indian Point. After the original Hudson River Day Company went out of business in 1948 another company continued the service to Indian Point. In the foreground of the top photograph and in the bottom photograph the *Miss Indian Point* speed boat is shown. For 75 cents visitors could take a ride on one. The best part of the trip came at its end when the boat sped into the dock only turning at the second to avoid a collision. *Courtesy of Town of Buchanan William J. Burke Historical Room.*

Indian Point Park

South of the piers was a 70 X 100 foot long dance pavilion called Assembly Hall. The building was open-aired to allow river breezes to enter. On weekends a dance band sailed to Indian Point on one of the steamers and played at the hall. *Courtesy of Town of Buchanan William J. Burke Historical Room.*

South of the dance hall were two Indian tepees. Chief Eagle Plume and two squaws lived there. They sold Indian Point souvenirs like feather headdresses, cards, blankets, and knives. *Courtesy of Town of Buchanan William J. Burke Historical Room.*

Indian Point Park

These two photographs are part of a panorama that is hanging in the William J. Burke Historical Room. They show part of the amusement area at Indian Point Park. In the top photograph a swing and the Caterpillar ride can seen. The group of people below is standing in front of a carousel. The sign in this photograph says rides were ten cents each or three for 25 cents. *Courtesy of Town of Buchanan William J. Burke Historical Room.*

Lost Amusement Parks of the Hudson Valley

The Little Dipper, a small roller coaster, was one of the rides for younger children. The cost was fourteen cents for children and twenty cents for adults. Below is a photograph of the fire engine ride. Children (possibly from the St. Joseph's Home) enjoy their ride. Behind the fire engine is what appears to be Tilt-a-Whirl. *Courtesy of Town of Buchanan William J. Burke Historical Room.*

Indian Point Park

Two other rides are shown in these photographs. The one above shows the rocket ship ride. Behind the rocket ship is a classic truck ride. An amusement park staple, the House of Horror thrilled old and young alike. *Courtesy of Town of Buchanan William J. Burke Historical Room.*

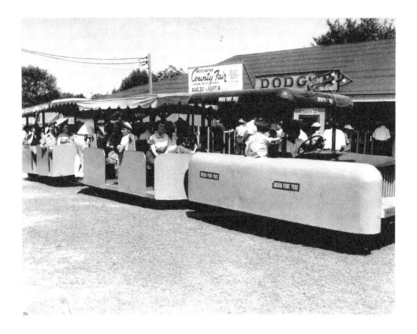

In 1952 and 1953 the Westchester County Fair was held at Indian Point Park. Kelmans wanted to revive the tradition of county fairs in Westchester. This fair was sponsored by the Westchester Horticultural and Agricultural Association. Behind the tram is a ride called Dodgem. Dodgem was a bumper car ride. This ride cost twenty five cents. *Courtesy of Town of Buchanan William J. Burke Historical Room.*

Indian Point Park

The last major event ever held at Indian Point Park was the Cristiani Brothers Circus in 1956. The Cristianis began their circus careers as bareback riders for Ringling Brothers. In 1949 the family started its own circus which, by 1958, was the second largest circus in North America. In 1960, circus economics forced them to close their own circus. The family is still in the circus business entertaining as a part of other circuses around the world. *Courtesy of Town of Buchanan William J. Burke Historical Room.*

The Cristiani Brothers Circus was a three ring operation. These photographs show some of the animals that were part of their show. *Courtesy of Town of Buchanan William .Burke Historical Room.*

Indian Point Park

In October 1954 Emanuel Kelmans sold Indian Point Park to the Consolidated Edison Gas and Electric Company for $250,000. By 1962 Indian Point I was generating electricity. The top picture shows the start of construction for the nuclear generating plant. The photograph below shows an aerial view of the construction site. At the top edge the athletic fields are still visible. The rectangle below them is the ruins of the swimming pool. *Above courtesy of Town of Buchanan William J. Burke Historical Room; below courtesy of Brian Vangor.*

This photograph shows Indian Point's three nuclear reactors at the present time. *Courtesy of Brian Vangor.*

One of the few remaining artifacts from Indian Point Park is this a sign pointing to the park. The sign is presently in a glass cabinet at the William J. Burke Historical Room. *Courtesy of Town of Buchanan William J. Burke Historical Room.*

Fort George Amusement Park

If one were to list all of Manhattan's many varied assets, amusement parks would not be among them. But there was a time, before the island's real estate became so valuable, when a large amusement area flourished for many years.

The Fort George amusement area in the Washington Heights section of northern Manhattan was just a short boat ride away from the confluence of the Harlem and Hudson Rivers at Spuyten Duyvil Creek. The creek separates Manhattan and the Bronx. The amusement area is rarely mentioned along with the likes of Coney Island and the Palisades Amusement

Park. But at its peak, Fort George competed with both of those historic parks. It remains the largest open-air amusement park in Manhattan's history. Perhaps its abrupt demise in 1913, after only an 18-year run, denied the area its proper spot in the canon of the amusement industry giants.

The term Fort George refers to a strategic fortification constructed in northern Manhattan during the American Revolution. Revolutionary soldiers bravely engaged the British from the fort shortly after the Battle of Brooklyn in 1776, allowing General George Washington and his army an escape route to Westchester and New Jersey. Though Washington escaped successfully, the British continued its stronghold in New York City and eventually rebuilt Fort George. With the signing of the Treaty of Paris in 1783, the British abandoned the fort. It will be remembered as the last colonial position to fall on the island of Manhattan. Today George Washington High School occupies the site.

In 1895, on and adjacent to the same hallowed grounds, a large and spectacular amusement area began to evolve. Some felt it would rival the hugely successful Steeplechase Park at Coney Island that opened in 1897. The location was ideal – perched atop cliffs along Amsterdam Avenue starting at 190th Street. Its western boundary was Audubon Avenue. The entertainment zone stretched north up to Fort George Avenue at least to 197th Street where the Curve Music Hall was located, though most of the amusement rides were situated a few blocks south. At roughly 1000 feet above sea level, the vistas looking across the Harlem

Fort George Amusement Park

River were breathtaking. Some of the rides were designed to take advantage of the location's natural terrain to enhance thrills.

As with most other amusement parks of the era, trolley transportation was crucial. In the case of Fort George, the Third Avenue Railway System, which connected the Bronx to Manhattan, was the conduit. With a terminal near Fort George, the line delivered locals and residents from throughout the city to the park's doorstep for the sum of five cents from most Manhattan locations. The nearby Westinghouse Power and Electric Company provided the electricity for the park using alternating current. Eventually, Con Edison, which used direct current, would buy out Westinghouse.

Initially, the amusement area was an amalgam of hastily assembled structures to house sideshows, fortune tellers, smaller rides, shooting galleries, penny arcades, and food concessions. Concessions were individually owned largely by German businessmen. Many had been concessionaires on the Upper East Side's Jones's Wood, a popular working class resort featuring beer gardens and many forms of entertainment. When that area was consumed by fire in 1894, the displaced entrepreneurs gravitated to the Fort George area along Amsterdam Avenue.

By 1899, a hotel and casino owned by John F. Schultheis was operating on the crest of the hill on Fort George Avenue. It eventually was heavily damaged by fire the date of which remains unclear. The Great Handicap Race Track just north of Fort George Avenue opened before the turn of the century as did the Harlem River Speedway which ran from what is now the Harlem River Drive from 155th Street to Dyckman Street. It featured equestrian races run by the well-healed that helped to attract more people to the growing amusement area. It wasn't until 1919 that the roadway opened for motorists. In 1922 it was paved for the first time.

However, it wasn't until the arrival of the Schenck brothers, Joseph and Nicholas, that the amusement area achieved premier status. Joseph and Nicholas Schenck became, by far, the park's major players. The Schencks emigrated from Russia in 1893 when Nicholas was 11 years old and Joseph was two years older. As very young men, their business acumen grew, yielding several successful small businesses. Joseph bought and operated a pharmacy where he had worked earlier as a lad. While visiting the bustling amusement area one weekend during 1904 they quickly realized that there was money to made at Fort George. They quickly established a modest sized (15 by 25 foot) drinking establishment called the Old Barrel. They were rewarded with success in more ways than they probably ever imagined.

They soon befriended a customer at the Old Barrel by the name of Marcus Loew. Loew had already achieved some fame and fortune as an owner of penny arcades, nickelodeons, and theaters in New Jersey and New York, including the Royal Theater in Brooklyn. The trio built a vaudeville stage adjacent to the Old Barrel which garnered even more profit. A cane board and knife board were added in the second season.

Fort George Amusement Park

Loew, also seeing the potential at Fort George, agreed to lend Nicholas and Joseph the funds necessary to construct a separate entertainment complex to be named Paradise Park at the Fort George amusement area in 1905. The Fort George Amusement Company was organized on February 8, 1905 listing Joseph Schenck as president, Marcus Loew as vice president, Nicholas Schenck as treasurer, and William Mundt as secretary. Initial capital assets were listed as $40,000. These events, along with the contributions of scores of other entrepreneurs, would lead to the amusement area being dubbed "Manhattan's Coney Island".

The thrilling rides and other recreational diversions at Paradise Park became wildly popular and spurred even more growth at the park. Only a power failure on August 9, 1905 marred the first season. The entire park went dark. Passengers in the top cars of the giant Ferris wheel panicked in the darkness on the crowded weekend night. Their screams could be heard throughout the park. Some threatened to jump and had to be restrained by fellow riders. People inside the Old Mill had no means of escape in the dark tunnels. Its boats remained still in the water as water ceased to flow inside the ride. Fortunately, a gunboat and several yachts in the river, realizing the emergency, shone their search lights on the park which alleviated further panic. Power was eventually restored and there were no casualties.

While the Schenck brothers maintained ownership in Paradise Park at Fort George, they formed another company, the Palisades Realty and Amusement Company in February 1910 through which they purchased the Palisades Amusement Park in Cliffside Park, New Jersey (rechristened the Schenck Brothers' Palisade Park). The Schencks used some of the proceeds from the sale of their vaudeville stage operation at Fort George to finance the purchase. They revitalized the New Jersey park with the construction of some of the largest rides in the area and the nation's largest salt water wave pool. Also, by 1910 Nicholas Schenck was listed in city records as a board officer on no less than a dozen corporations including his vice presidency of the Fort George Amusement Company.

By around 1920, they had begun to lose interest in the day-to-day operations of Palisades Amusement Park, and with Fort George's closure around 1914, they turned their focus instead to the growing film industry in Hollywood. They eventually sold their interest in the Palisades Amusement Park in 1935 to the Rosenthal brothers, who had enjoyed a modicum of success at Coney Island. Both Loew and the Schenck brothers went on to make fortunes in Hollywood. Joseph Schenck became Board Chairman of United Artists. He later founded 20th Century Fox along with Darryl Zanuck. Loew's Incorporated became a hugely successful chain of movie theaters. Nicholas Schenck was Loew's Incorporated's president and general manager and later became the head of Metro-Goldwyn-Mayer.

Around the time Paradise Park was gaining a foothold at Fort George, two hugely successful figures in the amusement industry, Elmer "Skip" Dundy and Frederic Thompson, made a splash with some startling news. Thompson and Dundy were best known for developing and building the sensational Luna Park and the Hippodrome at Coney Island. On March 31, 1906, they announced to the press that they would be building, in their words, an "immense amusement empire unlike anything in existence" and an "uptown wonderland" at Fort George. It would be called Vanity Fair.

Based on the 17th century classic *Pilgrim's Progress* by John Bunyan, the theme park, as they envisioned it, would be an architectural and amusement colossus with typical marketplaces of that era. The centerpiece would have been an extravaganza of a show featuring decoratively dressed chorus girls, majestic fountains, and "modern" lighting effects. They even went so far as to take out a 25 year lease on the Jennings Estate, the equivalent of 100 city lots. Plans were drawn up to construct an electric railway from the foot of the Dyckman Street station that eventually would wend its way up to Audobon Avenue.

Skip Dundy died suddenly on February 5, 1907 ending a most colorful life. But that did not deter Fred Thompson from moving forward with plans at Fort George. He made a startling announcement on March 26, 1907. Thompson announced plans for the construction of an airship terminal at Fort George. Airships 90 feet in length would dock at Fort George atop a 100-foot high platform. Passengers would ascend an elevator to the platform. The ships would float to a stop at a terminal atop buildings at Broadway and 29th Street. From there the journey would continue to Coney Island where the passengers would be met by a band atop the "Trip to the Moon" attraction. Thompson could cash in on both ends of the airships' journeys.

However, contractually the pair was prevented from opening enterprises in Manhattan. To circumvent that legal restriction, he and Dundy had stepped down as directors and officers of the Hippodrome and Luna Park. They were permitted to maintain a heavy financial investment in their Coney Island interests.

Alas, Vanity Fair was never built. But the names Thompson and Dundy did crop up again at Fort George. A small park under the pair's names opened at Fort George in June 1907. The feature attraction was Bostock's "Rounders" considered to be one of the most elaborate carousels in the world. Also scheduled to open were a figure-eight toboggan, a miniature railroad, and a cycle swing. The fate of the concession is unknown.

The pair had made fortunes but had spent a lion's share of it on yachts, enormous restaurant tabs, drinking, and other indulgences and extravagances. Skip Dundy's passing left Thompson awash in a sea of lofty ambitions and complicated finances. It is possible that Thompson just gave up on Fort George as finances became more pressing and he missed his partner's relative stability. Thompson never paid rent on the Fort George property and was in arrears to the tune of $150,000 when a list of his creditors was drawn up. Besides, Fort George was beginning to look like a risky investment at this juncture considering its limited

Fort George Amusement Park

space for expansion. His drinking problems worsened and he eventually lost Luna Park to creditors. Although he subsequently attempted several smaller ventures, he filed for bankruptcy in 1912. He died in 1919. Friends had to take up a collection to purchase a headstone.

But with Paradise Park on its enclosed three acre site and other operations in full swing starting in 1905, the Fort George amusement area still had something to please almost every taste judging by the crowds it drew. Up to 100,000 visitors per day, according to a 1907 newspaper account, arrived by trolley or horse and buggy. Local residents merely walked to the midway. Its features included two highly visible Ferris wheels, tunnel boat rides, skating rinks, a toboggan coaster that slithered down the cliff toward the Harlem River, swimming pools, and two other world-class roller coasters to please enthusiasts of that genre. Three beautiful carousels entertained young and old. Two of the carousels were built expressly for Fort George by the renowned Philadelphia Toboggan Company. One was commissioned in 1905 and another in 1908. In addition, countless midway concessions lined Amsterdam Avenue.

One coaster, built in 1907 was aptly nicknamed the "Rough Rider". It replaced a tamer coaster which operated from the opening year of Paradise Park. The original coaster was not bereft of problems. During its construction a worker was killed and several more were seriously injured when some pilings collapsed on March 28, 1905. The Rough Rider's run was checkered as well. The third-rail coaster required a motorman to operate it. In essence, it was akin to a subway ride in open-air cars hurtling down the side of the hill with figure eights and hairpin turns to make it more "interesting". Electric motors would haul the cars back up the hill after its run. It is doubtful even its builder, William Mengals of Coney Island fame, realized the thrills he created for the price of ten cents. The thrill ride lasted two and one half minutes on a track seventh eights of a mile long. Its maximum height was 75 feet.

According to reports, some motormen had a diabolical streak. Instead of coasting or slowing down over or around certain curves and hills as they were instructed to do, some pushed forward on the lever. Riders often got the thrill ride of their lives. Unfortunately, some were injured as they were thrown from the cars. Lawsuits abounded. After the first fire to strike Fort George Amusement Park in 1911, the Rough Rider was dismantled and reopened as a new attraction at the Schenck Brothers' Palisade Park. Interestingly, the ride ran in reverse of its operation at Fort George. The ride began at the base of the cliff until it reached the top, then the thrills began.

Mengals also designed the "Tickler" at Fort George, a tame ride by comparison. The ride, introduced by Mengals at Coney Island, was "designed to jostle, jolt, and jounce its riders about in their seats when the ride was in motion", according to its inventor. The bumping and whirling of the cars down an incline careening off rubber obstacles like a pinball machine created a fair amount of body contact. This

Fort George Amusement Park

action led to it being called "the perfect date ride for couples".

Vaudeville shows and dancing were popular at Fort George. At least four music halls, the Trocadero at 190th Street, the Star at 192nd Street (near the rear entrance to Paradise Park), Paradise Park Music Hall and, at the northern reaches of the entertainment zone, the Curve at 197th Street (probably named after the curve in Amsterdam Avenue leading to Fort George Avenue) offered quality vaudeville and musical acts at Fort George. The Trocadero's acts were provided by agents Sam and Freeman Bernstein. The Star was operated by C.J. Johne and its six-piece orchestra was a popular draw. There was no admission charge for the Paradise Music Hall. Profits were generated through the sale of food and refreshments. Featured regular performers at Fort George included the popular Professor Ziegler and his German band.

The midway was no less entertaining with its nine saloons, five shooting galleries, and the omnipresent freak sideshows. Among the sideshow attractions were the "Human Ostrich" and "Rameses the Giant Killer of the Zambesi". The former amazed patrons by swallowing items ranging from a pack of tacks to curled rancid sandwiches left out on the park's picnic tables. Rameses, a huge man who displayed feats of strength, was said to have escaped unaided from a horde of Italian soldiers. Children were able to enjoy the pony track, the roller rink, or the open-air swimming pool. When their parents wished to be alone for a spell, a facility was available for supervision of the tots (for a fee).

A large rink hosted roller skaters in the summer and, it is believed, ice skaters in the winter. It debuted in time for the opening of the 1907 season. In June 1907, a most unusual wedding was held at the rink. Raymond Barrett and his 19 year old fiancé Susan Pierce first met at the rink. In celebration of that event, they, along with the minister, laced on roller skates for the ceremony that took place on the rink's floor. Rings exchanged, the newlyweds were joined on the floor by 500 couples. They all skated to "Love Me and the World is Mine". They honeymooned in Atlantic City.

Restaurants and other food concessions were kept busy by the influx of visitors, particularly on the weekends. One popcorn and candy (taffy was a specialty) concession at Fort George was owned and operated by Mary Gish, mother of legendary movie queen Lillian Gish. Lillian's father had left the family before she could even form memories of him. Mary Gish went about saving what money she could from a small business in Brooklyn and some sporadic acting work in order to purchase the space at the park in the summer of 1905. According to her memoirs, Lillian's job at the age of 11 or 12 was to stand on a box and repeat over and over in as plaintive a voice as possible, "Would you like to buy some candy?"

Lillian also reminisced about the day her younger sister Dorothy went missing among the hubbub at Fort George. Frantically, the family searched among all the stands and stalls until they spotted her standing high on the snake charmer's platform during a performance. Pushing through the gathered crowd,

Fort George Amusement Park

Mary nearly fainted when she saw a huge snake wrapped around her daughter's body. Little Dorothy was smiling and appeared oblivious to the snake. She was duly punished.

When business at the candy stand was slow, the girls exercised the ponies at Mr. Craemer's pony concession... bareback and fast. One day little Dorothy fell off her pony. She was rushed to the hospital where she was treated for a compound fracture of her arm. Meanwhile Lillian, left behind at the park, feared the worst had befallen her sister. It was evening before Mary returned from the hospital with Dorothy and no one could find Lillian. Concerned workers at Fort George had been scouring the area a better part of the day. Finally Mary discovered the terrified Lillian crouching in the machinery shed at the center of a carousel. She quickly reassured her daughter that everything was going to be all right. Lillian claimed that her early horseback riding at Fort George spurred a love of that skill that endured throughout her storied life.

But after two years, the Gish concession burned to the ground leaving the family with little income. Reluctantly, Mary returned to acting and strongly encouraged her young daughter to do so as well. The rest is history.

Improvements to the area were made in 1906 and 1907 to ensure that patronage would grow. A *Variety* article indicating that a "sprucing up" was needed perhaps spurred many of the changes. Another Ferris wheel, topping out at 70 feet and with 16 passenger cars, appeared on the scene in 1906. By the 1907 season the Rough Rider was in place. A 30 foot-slide at Paradise Park was added late in the year. Speed and Darcy's "Old Mill" was refurbished with new effects inside the darkened cavern. Several of the dance halls expanded. More lights illuminated the area much to the chagrin of nearby residents. An elevator installed by the Reno Inclined Elevator Company was already in place. No longer would patrons be required to scale the steep steps from Amsterdam Avenue up the hill to Audobon Avenue. Fresh coats of paint renewed many visible areas. In addition, a parking garage was added for those fortunate enough to own a vehicle. The crowds continued to come.

Petty crimes had plagued the area for several years. Things were brought under control when the 152nd Precinct, under the direction of newly-assigned Sergeant Patrick Corcoran, instituted changes in patrols along peripheral areas and cracked down on swindling concessionaires. To appease local residents, the area was closed by 11 P.M. every evening starting in September 1908.

In June 1908 plans were filed by Fred Thompson for a "roli rider", a circle wheeler with a 32-foot diameter platform built of wood and steel at a cost of $3,000. It would accommodate 66 riders at a time who would be spun around six times per minute. Thompson planned to lease the ride for the season. Since no images exist of the ride, it is unclear if it came to fruition especially considering Thompson's decline.

Fort George Amusement Park

The clientele at the Fort George Amusement Park was generally considered more working-class than Coney Island's attendees. But nonetheless, respectable behavior was expected. Two of its fine hotels, the Fort George Hotel and Casino and the Fort Wendel Hotel and Café, catered to some wealthier guests, many of whom enjoyed the gambling and fine food offered. Fort Wendel, located at 194th Street and the east side of Amsterdam Avenue, was a popular spot that featured an all-ladies orchestra. It burned around 1907. But as the area entered the second decade of the century, the character of its visitors began to change.

Women, whether alone or even in groups, had always felt secure at Fort George. Suddenly, many reports of harassment, and worse, surfaced. People were no longer dressing in their Sunday's finest. Local residents became increasingly concerned about noise, rowdiness, and public intoxication. Petty crimes were mounting again. In the fall of 1909, even the local police precinct located on 152nd Street suggested to city officials that the park should be shuttered. Concurrently, the Schencks were probably beginning to focus their efforts on their New Jersey amusement park and other enterprises out of town.

Also around this time, real estate speculators were eyeing the area for housing development. They felt that the amusement area was an obstacle to their interests. Local residents lobbied for the construction of a public park but the speculators fought that notion realizing the possibility of huge profits as real estate values soared in Manhattan. The city rejected the idea of a park stating that it was not in a strong enough financial position to lose the tax revenue that the amusement park generated. The city's response was supported with figures including the fact that many schools were already facing class sizes of up to 60 children in that very neighborhood. In any event, some construction of new buildings began along the perimeter of the amusement area.

Calling it an "immoral" resort at a meeting on February 26, 1910, members of the Washington Heights Taxpayers Association, acting on behalf of several civic groups, once again petitioned that the amusement area be razed. It was no surprise that developers fully backed the group. Nearby residents raised their voices in protest over the squeals and groans of the Ferris wheels, the cacophony of carousel music, the "hilarity" of the dance halls, fireworks, and the bright lights burning late on the weekends. Safety and sleepless nights were the crux of their issues.

On December 10, 1911, an arsonist attempted to burn the park down. The suspect was quickly spotted by a local resident who took chase but was unable to collar the culprit under the cloak of darkness. His motive will never be known. The wind-blown flames destroyed the Star Music Hall (formerly the historic Star Hotel dating back to colonial times), the Fort George Hotel, Paradise Park's dance hall, a popular tavern, and some smaller concessions. The three-alarm blaze also threatened the nearby Isabella Geriatric Home. Despite the setback, the 1912 season opened as scheduled.

Fort George Amusement Park

The park's fatal blow came on June 9, 1913. Another suspicious fire, described by many fire officials as the most "spectacular" they had ever seen, nearly destroyed the entire amusement park in the early morning hours. The Paradise Park night watchman, Dominick Barnot, quickly reported that several buildings were ablaze but he was too late. Within ten minutes, another dance hall outside of Paradise Park was fully engulfed in flames that were already soaring more than 100 feet into the air. The conflagration was eventually observed as far south as 42nd Street. Citizens across the river in the Morris Heights section of the Bronx spilled out of their homes to view the spectacle. Spared only were some of the smaller amusement areas, a few food concessions, the pool, one carousel, and a billiards parlor.

Firefighters, realizing that they could not stave off the inferno at the park, allowed the park's grand structures to burn. They turned their attention to nearby residential and business buildings instead. Thousands descended upon the Fort George area, despite the early hour, to view the inferno. Nearby tenants formed bucket brigades to toss water on their roofs to prevent the sparks from igniting their buildings. First to collapse were the roller coasters, followed by the giant Ferris wheels, the carousels, and the skating rink. At one hundred feet high, the largest Ferris wheel succumbed early and the flames were seen for miles around until it collapsed. All of the structures at Paradise Park were either destroyed or severely damaged. Except for the few that were spared (including one of the carousels) at the rest of the park, all the structures were fully engulfed in flames within 30 minutes. On the day after the fire, thousands roamed the park's acreage to observe the changed landscape and the smoldering remains and to scavenge for mementos.

Barely had the last embers extinguished when Joseph Schenck announced to the press on June 14 that he would rebuild Paradise Park. It would not only be grander but he proposed building a giant roof over a good portion of the park so visitors could come and enjoy the amusements rain or shine. He would have it ready by the following season. Community protests against rebuilding grew leading to news headlines such as "Citizens Fight New (Amusement) Park" in the *New York Sun* on September 25, 1913.

The concept of a public park was brought up again but the city maintained its stance that tax revenue could not be sacrificed.

The Schencks' lease on Paradise Park was due to expire around this time. It is doubtful anyone will ever know if they had truly planned to stay on. Some reports suggest that the brothers transported salvaged remnants from Fort George to the Schenck Brothers' Palisade Park. Nobody else came forth with any plans to resurrect the park. Some smaller businesses probably struggled on for awhile into 1914. A movement by local concerned citizens' groups finally led to the cancellation of all licenses and leases at the Fort George amusement area.. The clean up of the area was "brought about with no small difficulty" according to a *New York Times* account. The amusement area's land would stay in limbo for a number of years. Eventually parcels of land were sold. The owner of Thom's Scenic Railway sold his 100 by 228 foot parcel, all equipment included, at public auction for $25,000 on January 27, 1916.

The Schenck brothers retained some property at Amsterdam Avenue and 193rd Street. In August 1917, they floated the idea of building two large movie studio buildings under their still viable Fort George Amusement Company, of which Marcus Loew remained an original partner. A newspaper account on December 29 again reiterated their desire. The project never got off the ground.

Interestingly, a newspaper account on July 26, 1919 indicated that some of the amusement area's unsold acreage was being used as a public vegetable garden. One hundred fifty separate garden plots were tended by volunteers. On a somber note, it was reported that some of the bean and squash plants' vines grew on a trellis that was the remains of one of the amusement area's carousel houses.

With the amusement area now just a memory, local groups lobbied for a new high school to be built on the spot of historic Fort George. Despite much debate and competition from other interested areas of Manhattan, they prevailed. The new George Washington High School became a reality in 1925. Its distinguished alumni include news reporter Edwin Newman, opera singer Maria Callas, former Secretary of State Henry Kissinger, famed economist Alan Greenspan, singer Harry Belafonte, and athletes Rod Carew and Manny Ramirez.

In 1928, the City of New York purchased the remaining tracts of the former amusement park's grounds east of Amsterdam Avenue. The city eventually extended Highbridge Park northward to fill the void. Today's park is starkly tranquil compared to the fervor and excitement on the grounds around a century ago. Remarkably, no historic signs or plaques mark the spot where the amusement park brought enjoyment to so many.

Interestingly, the amusement area's lone carousel that survived the great fire of 1913 has been preserved. Until 2009 it was a centerpiece attraction at the Palisades Center shopping mall in West Nyack, New York, where it operated for 11 years. An organ that played for one of the carousels has been lovingly preserved and now resides in England. These are the only treasures known today to exist from the Fort George era.

Fort George Amusement Park

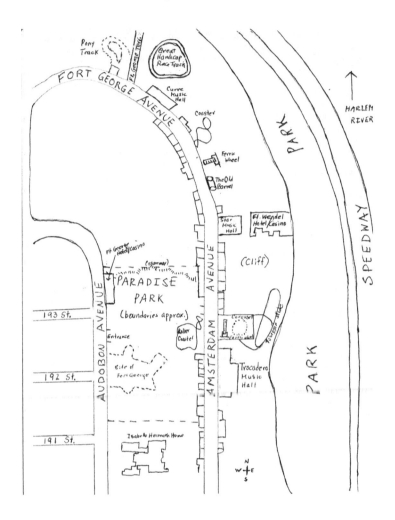

This map represents the Fort George entertainment zone's know attractions. The location of other amusements is uncertain. *Map drawn by Wes Gottlock.*

Lost Amusement Parks of the Hudson Valley

Although the Fort George Amusement Park was comprised of many individual concessionaires Joseph Schenck, pictured here, and his brother Nicholas were the driving force behind Paradise Park, the entertainment zone's largest enterprise. After much success with amusement parks, the brothers turned their attention to the booming film industry in Hollywood where they made their fortunes. Joseph Schenck married film star Norma Talmadge.

The Schencks started humbly at Fort George. They established the Old Barrel, a drinking establishment perched on a cliff overlooking the Harlem River. They opened the Old Barrel in mid-summer 1903 and cleared $1,200 in just a few weeks. By adding free vaudeville acts (aided by Marcus Loew) they netted $16,000 in their second year of operation. *Courtesy of Jason Minter.*

Fort George Amusement Park

Marcus Loew befriended the Schenck brothers while on a visit to Fort George. The trio was intrigued by the possibilities for profit there. Marcus Loew helped front the funds necessary for the Schencks to build Paradise Park. The three men partnered in many other businesses even after their arrival in Hollywood. Loew's chain of theaters became hugely profitable.

While this postcard is labeled as the entrance to the Old Fort or Mystic Cave, it remains unknown exactly what awaited the patrons inside. It's possible the Mystic Cave was an attraction modeled after Steeplechase Park's Cave at Coney Island, a ride through a dark tunnel with fans emulating strong winds. *Courtesy of Jason Minter.*

This is one of two entry points to Paradise Park (one on Amsterdam Avenue, the other on Audobon Avenue). Note the signs advertising the roller skating rink. Aerial swings (also called airplane swings) were a staple item at amusement parks of the era. The one in the upper right seemed to be taller than most. *Author's collection.*

Fort George Amusement Park

The Rough Rider was a third-rail powdered coaster which had a checkered history at Fort George. While it provided many thrills along the cliff, it also created many problems. It was eventually removed to the Schenck Brothers' Palisade Park in New Jersey.

The entertainment zone ran for a number of blocks along Amsterdam Avenue into Fort George Avenue. Part of Paradise Park can be seen on the left. Fort George was essentially a "trolley park" served by the Third Avenue line. The Fort Wendel Hotel and Café (194th Street) is off to the right. The view is looking uptown.

In the preceding picture, "Moxie" occupies a few billboard spaces. Moxie was a popular drink created in Lowell, Massachusetts in 1878. Its strong rich flavor promised renewed vigor and verve and was originally marketed as a medicine. The expression "having moxie" is derived from the brand name. It implies courage and aggressiveness. Incredibly, it is still produced in the northeast and it is the state beverage of Maine.

Fort George Amusement Park

The entertainment zone at Fort George probably ended around 197th Street where the Curve Music Hall was located. The signage above the awning represented a lager beer produced by George Ehret. Ehret founded the Hell Gate Brewery on the upper east side of Manhattan in 1866. He produced a sophisticated lager beer which rivaled the best imports from Germany and for a time he was the nation's largest brewer.

Another postcard view shows Amsterdam Avenue in the 190s circa 1906. *Courtesy of Jason Miner.*

Lost Amusement Parks of the Hudson Valley

This postcard can be dated sometime between 1905 and early 1908. Looking across the Harlem River, the Fort George Amusement Park dominates the cliff. Paradise Park would be located on the extreme left. The Fort Wendel Hotel and Café (also known as the Fort Wendel Hotel and Amusement Resort) sits just to its right. The hotel was owned by a colorful figure, Captain Louis Wendel, who commanded the National Guard's First Battery Armory on West 66th Street. Wendel became a wealthy man but certainly not on his military income alone. In December 1906, Wendel was indicted on a litany of charges. Among them were taking kickbacks for jobs at the Armory, renting the Armory's horse stalls to private citizens, operating an illegal bar at the Armory, and padding expense accounts. In addition, he was accused of cheating tenants of buildings he owned in the Bronx. Wendel was discharged by court martial in 1907. The Fort Wendel Hotel and Café burned shortly thereafter. He died in 1914. *Author's collection.*

Fort George Amusement Park

This circa 1905 view shows the lower (or "downtown") end of the amusement area before the Rough Rider was built along the cliff. The park was lit up brightly at night much to the consternation of neighborhood residents. *Courtesy of Jason Minter.*

Another view across the Harlem River shows the Rough Rider coaster (to the left) in place. It was built for Paradise Park probably in 1905. *Author's collection.*

Lost Amusement Parks of the Hudson Valley

One entry point to the Fort George Hotel and Casino was located on the west side of Amsterdam Avenue. The hotel was located was located at the top of the hill near Amsterdam Avenue. It was destroyed during a fire on December 10, 1911. *Courtesy of Jason Minter.*

Even the roller coaster in Paradise Park had a billboard of sorts. It states that the park's lighting was provided by the United Electric Company on Broadway. The Proctor's billboard referred to the theaters owned by Frederick Freeman Proctor, the "Dean of Vaudeville". Proctor was responsible for devising the first continuous circuit of vaudeville acts. In all he owned over 25 theaters, some of which still stand. *Courtesy of Jason Minter.*

Fort George Amusement Park

Shown in this postcard is the view of Morris Heights in the Bronx from the Fort George amusement area. Many citizens of Morris Heights decried the loud noise late into the night that carried across the water. Civic groups met and elected a representative, George Budlong, to meet with the Schencks and the owner of Thom's Scenic Railway. Budlong had previously spoken to Joseph Schenck and told the owner that for the sum of $75 he would report back to his committee that everything would be taken care of. Schenck immediately reported the bribe offer to the police. When Budlong came to the meeting to collect his money, two reporters, acting as employees of the park, witnessed the transfer of money. Mr. Budlong felt he was "set up" but his appeal fell on deaf ears. *Courtesy of Jason Minter.*

Lost Amusement Parks of the Hudson Valley

Four row Jumper. Extra Large Horses. Finely Carved Chariots. Ft. George, N.Y.

The only carousel known to survive the fires at Fort George was the PTC #15 manufactured by the renown Philadelphia Toboggan Company in 1908. It featured "jumping" horses in a four-abreast array across its 52 foot diameter. After Fort George's closure it turned up at Summit Lake Park in Akron, Ohio in 1918. Subsequent to that, it traveled to State Fair Park in West Allis, Wisconsin in 1924. In 1961 the carousel moved to Muskego Beach, Wisconsin. Clara and Duane Perron bought the PTC #15 in 1985. The Perrons performed extensive restoration work. It was then featured at the Vancouver World's Fair in 1986 and at the Puente Hills Mall in California. From 1998 until July of 2009 it was entertaining young and old at the Palisades Center Mall in West Nyack, New York. Soon it will be finding a new home at an old refurbished mill in Dee, Washington. It is a stunningly beautiful reminder of the Fort George Amusement Park glory days. *Courtesy of the Philadelphia Toboggan Company.*

This 1999 photograph shows Allison Travis and her son Jesse taking a spin on the PCT #15 at the Palisades Center Mall in West Nyack, New York. The identifying plaque can be observed in the upper right corner. *Photograph by Wes Gottlock.*

Here and There

While the preceding chapters highlight some of the larger lost amusement parks along the Hudson Valley, they are by no means an exhaustive list of places of enjoyment during the first half of the 20th century. Other locations, not necessarily amusement parks in the strict sense, served to meet the recreational needs of the valley's residents and its summer visitors, particularly from New York City.

In Westchester County along the northern shore of Croton Point, a small amusement park was established in 1923. Formerly the grounds housed a brickyard and later a winery both owned and operated by the Underhill family. The modest amusements at Croton Point Park consisted of a Ferris wheel, an aerial swing, small midway stalls, and a carousel. Ample

Here and There

picnic and bathing areas along the Hudson River added to the allure.

Rockland Lake, just west of the Hudson River and just north of Nyack, was the setting for an amusement area along the same scale as Croton Point and around the same time period. Just east of Rockland Lake, the base of Hook Mountain in Nyack provided visitors with a carousel, a dance pavilion, bathing in the Hudson, picnic areas, a playground, and scenic vistas. Now both Rockland Lake and Hook Mountain are part of the Palisades Interstate Park Commission's system.

Bear Mountain State Park and Harriman State Park in Rockland County were established around 1909. As the parks developed, they hosted many thousands of visitors each week. Boating, picnicking along pristine Hessian Lake, hiking, bathing, and eventually skiing and other winter sports could be enjoyed around its centerpiece, the historic Bear Mountain Inn. Steamships brought New York City visitors to these parks until automobiles became the preferred mode of transportation. Many visitors flocked to Rockland County also to enjoy the resorts and vaudeville entertainment in Spring Valley.

Further north and about 20 miles west of the Hudson River, Midway Park in Middletown in Orange County hosted in excess of 10,000 people on busy days. Established just before the turn of the 20th century, Midway Park was a creation of the Middletown-Goshen Traction Company. The trolley company established Midway Park roughly halfway between those two small cities. It was sometimes referred to as "the Coney Island of Middletown and Goshen". Among its many amusements, it featured a rather long scenic railway which snaked its way through a wooded area. A 75-foot lookout tower provided fun seekers with picturesque vistas on clear days. The park closed in 1924 when the Middletown-Goshen Traction Company's power plant failed. The company did not have the financial reserves to repair the damage. The Orange County Golf Club is currently situated just across from where the park was located.

Mount Beacon is located in Dutchess County on the east side of the Hudson River across from the city of Newburgh. It got its name from the "beacon" fires which burned on the top of the mountain during the Revolutionary War. All along the Hudson Highlands' mountain tops American soldiers, acting as lookouts, lit signal fires to warn of British movement along the Hudson River. On July 4, 1900, the Melzingah Chapter of the Daughters of the American Revolution dedicated a stone obelisk to commemorate the signal fires which had burned there.

The views from the top of Mount Beacon prompted Weldon F. Weston and Henry W. Coates to organize the Incline Railway Association in 1900. They hired the Otis Elevator Company of Yonkers, New York to design and build an incline railway. This railway would have the steepest incline of all its contemporaries (although this was later disputed). The average grade was 65 degrees with a maximum grade of 75 degrees. Construction was begun in the winter of 1901.

Here and There

Memorial Day 1902 marked the first trip up the mountain. By the end of the season, 60,000 people had ridden the funicular to the top of Mount Beacon. The owners felt that the panoramic views of the surrounding area, the history of the mountain, and the ride alone would not be enough to entice people back to the mountain top. They added a casino and the Beaconcrest Hotel atop the mountain.

Thousands took the Newburgh-Beacon ferry and the trolley to the base station of the incline. Many others came by day liners from New York or other river towns. Near the peak, at an elevation of 1,549 feet above sea level, the air was always ten degrees cooler than in the valley below. Visitors could pass the day picnicking, enjoying the entertainment, or dancing.

Cottages built on Mount Beacon allowed people to stay for extended periods or for the season near the mountain's summit. There were park-like walkways, fountains, a dancing hall, dining rooms, spacious balconies, and a roof top observatory equipped with telescopes.

On October 16, 1927 a fire destroyed both the casino and the Beaconcrest Hotel. All that remained was the powerhouse for the incline railway. Since the railway was still operational, the casino was quickly rebuilt. But before a new hotel could be constructed, the Great Depression set in. Plans for a new hotel were scrapped.

During the 1930s and 1940s, the nation was undergoing a series of crises. The Depression coupled with World War II created a tremendous decline in tourism. In addition there were two more fires, one in 1934 and a second in 1938 which destroyed sections of the track. But the railway recovered and continued operations. The number of paying customers, however, continued to wane. Only 20,000 to 30,000 people rode the rails in 1963.

Another fire destroyed the lower incline railway station and a railway car on November 10, 1967. Even though the railway continued to operate, the writing was on the wall. The operating company could not afford to make any capital improvements. By 1978, a tax sale of the mountain top resulted in the owners having to close their business. In September 1983, a cataclysmic fire burned the tracks from top to bottom, destroying both stations and the powerhouse atop the mountain. In 1995 and 1998, Scenic Hudson purchased parcels totaling 234 acres on the crest and slope of Mount Beacon.

Founded in 1996, the Mount Beacon Incline Railroad Restoration Society's goal is to "Restore, operate and preserve an integral piece of American industrial, engineering, transportation, and leisure history". The society, with the permission of Scenic Hudson, hopes to rebuild the incline railroad so that people may once again have easy access to the summit. Once there they too could enjoy the cooler temperatures and the awe-inspiring views of the Hudson Highlands as generations before did.

Almost 30 miles north of Beacon, the city of Kingston in Ulster County also had a riverside attraction. Kingston Point Park was established in 1896 by Samuel Decker Coykendall who had significant interests in the Ulster and Delaware Railroad and was president of the Cornell Steamboat Company. He extended the railroad to Kingston Point and built a pier so visitors could depart Day Line steamboats and take a train to the Catskills. He created the park by filling in a swamp and adding a lagoon and a man-made island, a Ferris wheel, bridges, a merry-go-round, shooting galleries, a tintype shop, several restaurants, and a dance hall. The island featured an elegant gazebo for concerts and it was the milieu for firework displays.

The Oriental Hotel opened on a bluff overlooking the park in 1899, and by 1903 nearly 1,000,000 attended the park during its season. Though its amusements were few and small in scope, the location was lovely. It was more relaxing than many of the larger amusement parks previously discussed. But in 1922 the Oriental Hotel burned down and the park went into a decline. By 1928, nothing was left of the park. Today part of the property is the called the Kingston Point Rotary Park. It still contains the original gate from the park's heyday. Pleasure seekers can still spend a fine day at the park even though the massive crowds, the trains, and the steamships are increasingly fading memories of the past.

Lost Amusement Parks of the Hudson Valley

This view of Mount Beacon was taken looking south. In the foreground the lower railway station can be seen. The incline had only two rails until it reached the turnout, or switch, which had four rails. The turnout enabled two tram cars to operate at the same time on one set of tracks. The casino is perched on the mountain top. *Courtesy of Carla Decker.*

Looking from the mountain top one can see the extremely steep incline (average of 65 degrees) that the railway needed to climb to the summit. Two cars can be seen halfway down the mountain. *Courtesy of Carla Decker.*

Here and There

This monument was dedicated on July 4, 1900 by the Daughters of the American Revolution. It is a monument recalling the signal or beacon fires that were lit on this mountain to warn General George Washington of the movement of the British during the Revolutionary War. The inset at the left shows the switch where the two tram cars could pass each other during their ascent and descent. The right inset and postcard below show the powerhouse for the railway and the casino at the top of Mount Beacon. *Courtesy of Carla Decker.*

Lost Amusement Parks of the Hudson Valley

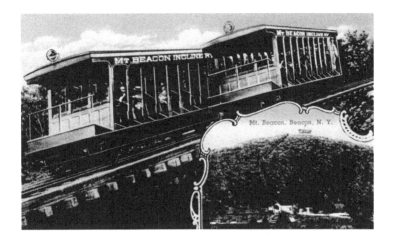

Two tram cars pass each other along the way. *Courtesy of Carla Decker.*

At the top of Mount Beacon, the Beaconcrest Hotel is seen on the left, the casino in the center, and the railroad's powerhouse on the right. Some of the walking trails appear in front of the structures. *Courtesy of Carla Decker.*

Here and There

The Hudson River Day Line's *New York*, built in 1887, pulls into the wharf at Kingston Point Park. *Courtesy of the Library of Congress.*

While Kingston Point was not a full-scale amusement park with many rides and attractions, it did have a carousel pictured above and a small Ferris wheel. There was enough to do for most folks to spend a pleasant day. *Author's collection.*

Kingston Point Park was a lovely spot in its heyday. On the left hand side of the photograph on the previous page the building with the American flag is Bennett's Restaurant. The Ferris wheel, other small shops, and the tintype gallery are on the right. Above the lagoon and the bridge leading to a man-made island which housed the gazebo for concerts and fireworks is seen. Boaters enjoyed paddling around the lagoon. *Courtesy of the Library of Congress.*

Here and There

The Oriental Hotel, the white building on the right, was built in 1899. The stately structure burned to the ground in 1992 at a time when the park started to decline. *Courtesy of the Library of Congress.*

The crowd in this photograph seems to be heading for the steamship in the background. Directly behind the gazebo is a large restaurant. Fortunately, the beautiful setting along the river can still be appreciated as the land was set aside for the creation of public parks. *Courtesy of the Library of Congress.*

Lost Amusement Parks of the Hudson Valley

Made in the USA
Middletown, DE
08 February 2019